GRAFFITI 4

THE EMPIRE WRITES BACK

Collected and compiled by Roger Kilroy
Wall-to-wall illustrations by
McLACHLAN

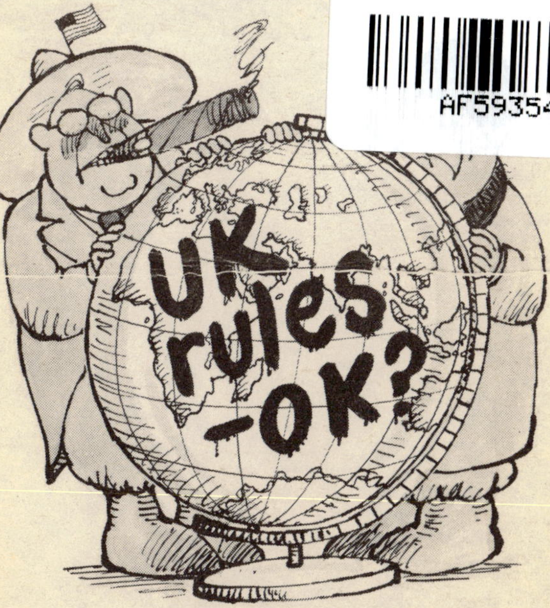

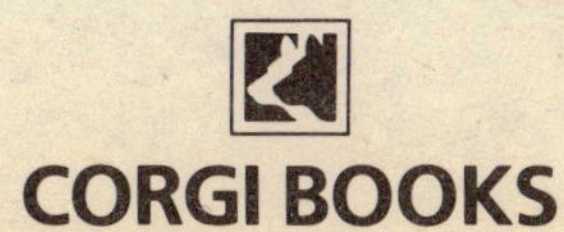

GRAFFITI 4: THE EMPIRE WRITES BACK
A CORGI BOOK 0 552 99022 1

First publication in Great Britain

PRINTING HISTORY

Corgi edition published 1983
Corgi edition reprinted 1984

Corgi Books are published by
Transworld Publishers Ltd.,
Century House, 61-63 Uxbridge Road,
Ealing, London W5 5SA.

Made and printed in Great Britain by the Guernsey Press Co. Ltd.,
Guernsey, Channel Islands.

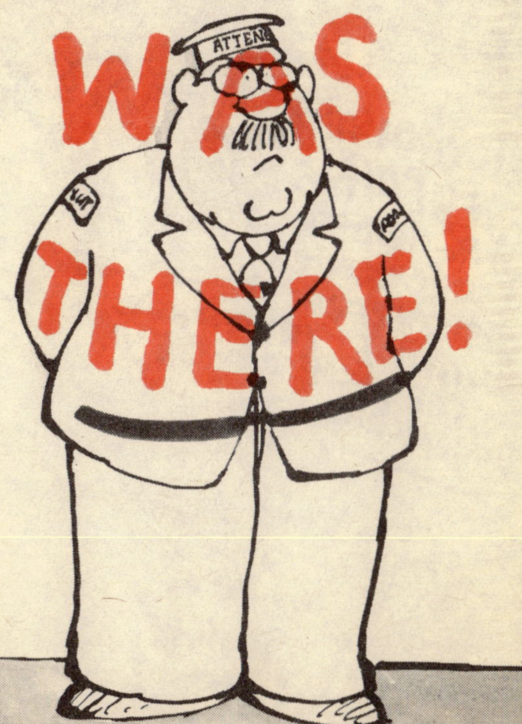
EXHIBITION OF GRAFFITI
THIS WAY
KILROY
WAS
THERE!

Also by Roger Kilroy and Edward McLachlan

GRAFFITI 1: THE SCRAWL OF THE WILD
GRAFFITI 2: THE WALLS OF THE WORLD
GRAFFITI 3: THE GOLDEN GRAFFITI AWARDS
GRAFFITI 5: AS THE ACTRESS SAID TO THE BISHOP
ILLUMINATED LIMERICKS
KISS ME, HARDY

and published by Corgi Books

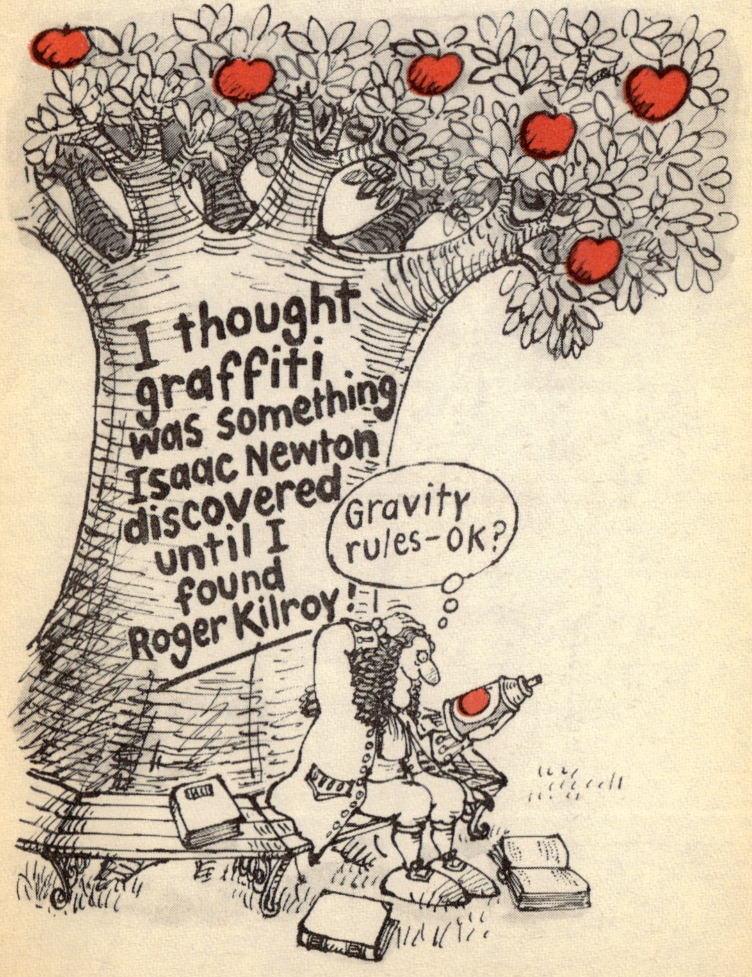

CONTENTS

WELCOME!

And thank you — not only for buying/begging/borrowing *The Empire Writes Back* when you must surely already own copies of *The Scrawl of the Wild* (Corgi, 1979), *The Walls of the World* (Corgi, 1980) and *The Golden Graffiti Awards* (Corgi, 1981), but also for making the new book possible. Yes, this latest anthology of wall-talk is entirely comprised of your contributions. From all over the world — from Port Stanley in the South to Glasgow in the North, from San Francisco in the West to Hackney in the East — you have sent us your favourite graffiti, and for the hundreds of letters, scores of postcards and two bricks, we are duly grateful.

We received particularly choice material from Chelmsford in Essex, from B.F.P.O. 20 in Dortmund, West Germany, from Albermarle Barracks in Newcastle-Upon-Tyne, and from Moonee Ponds, Victoria, Australia. And for especially memorable and generous contributions (e.g. they sent more than most) we would like to thank Susannah Hubert, Natasha Lee, John Allan, Mr. D. A. Connor, M. B. Sennett, Paul Wilson, Mr. R. A. Eales, Paul Ebbs, Margaret Finlayson, Gilbert Safarian, Martin Crouch, Mr. W. A. Brown, Peter Kealey, Lillith Ranson, Miss Sarah Smith, Darren Ellis, P. O. Dwyer, Ron Sainty, Mrs. June Addies, June Harris, Hazel Wright, Michael Butrovich, Scott Cameron, Mrs W. Maun, John Gwent, Steve Owen, Paul James, G. Workman, J. G. Davies, Adrian Pont, 24618082 J Sig. K. Joyce, Vance Hinkinson, Callum Chochrane, John May, Scott Brown, Miss Melanie Chesney, Paul Morris, Anthony Dure, Tim Schinkel, D. C. and J. E. Reeves, John Sherriff, Andrew Limond, Jnr., G. Brough, B. Wishart, and G. Caili and the Staff of the Mount Pleasant Hotel, London WC1.

May the Farce be with you.

WHAT THE EYE DOESN'T SEE, THE FEET WILL FALL OVER

I USED TO BE SCHIZOPHRENIC, BUT NOW I'M LONELY

SAY IT WITH FLOWERS – GIVE HER A TRIFFID!

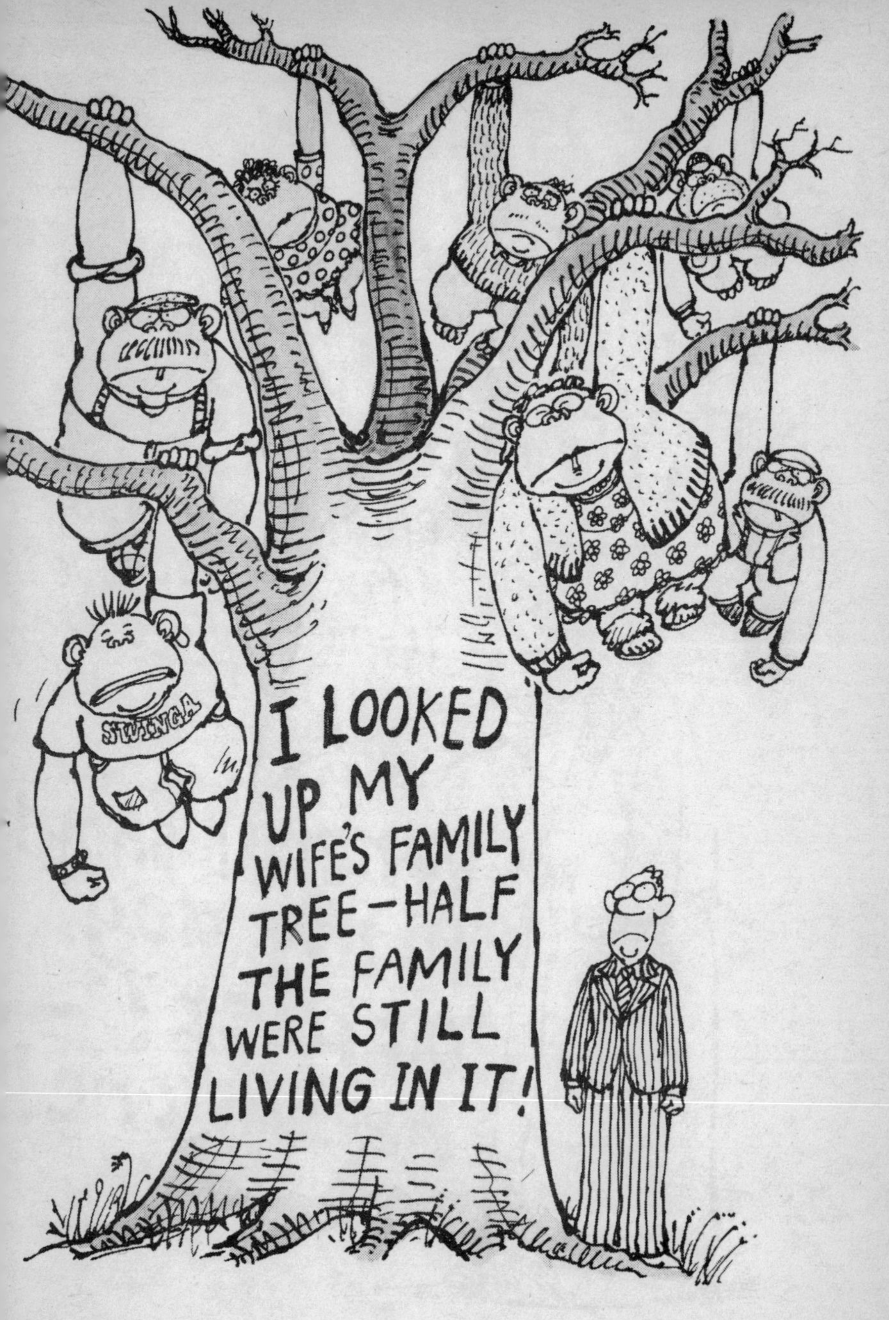
SWINGA
I LOOKED UP MY WIFE'S FAMILY TREE—HALF THE FAMILY WERE STILL LIVING IN IT!

LIFE IS LIKE AN ICE CREAM JUST WHEN YOU THINK YOU'VE GOT IT LICKED, IT DRIPS ALL OVER YOU!

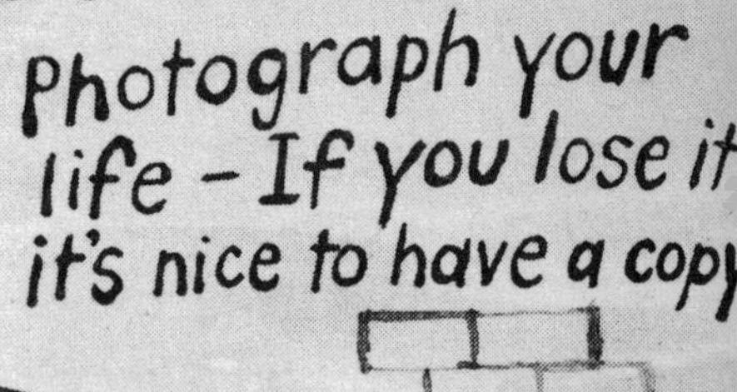

When I shout to my dog 'attack!' he has one!

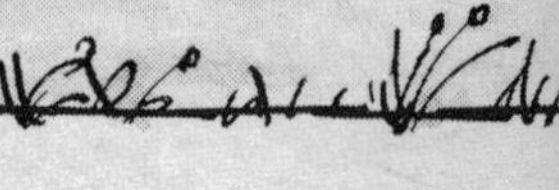

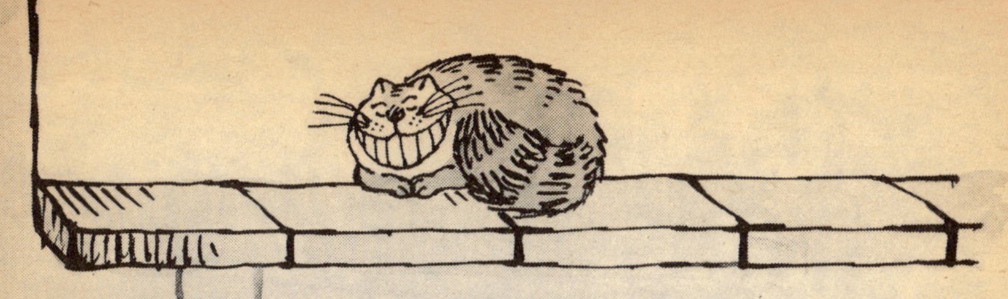

BUREAUCRACY RULES - O.K?
O.K?
O.K?

Jargon rules
-ongoing dominance
situation?

AMNESIA RULES — O

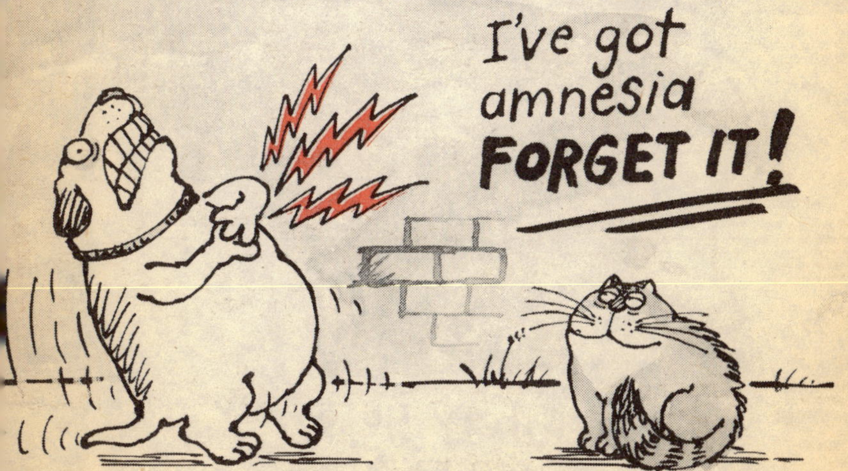

The cost of living is killing me

DON'T LET TURKEY BECOME ANOTHER CHILE - EAT MACARONI!

LIGHT UP AN EMBASSY — JOIN THE S.A.S

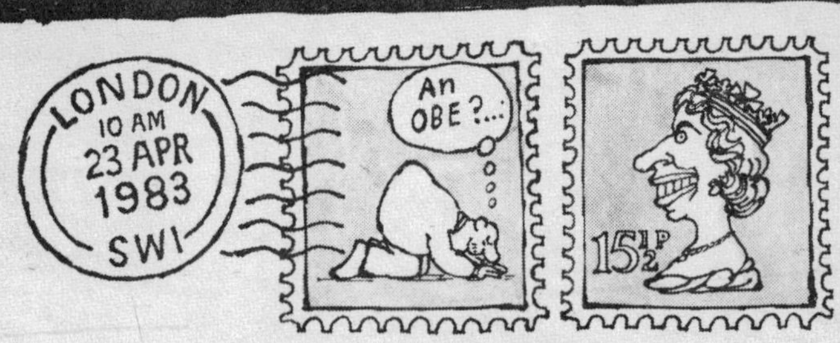

STAMP OUT PHILATELY!

No! Philately gets you everywhere!

WHY DO WOMEN SAY THEY'VE BEEN SHOPPING WHEN THEY HAVEN'T BOUGHT ANYTHING?

The M1 is not all it's cracked up to be.

Eat figs and prunes — start a movement!

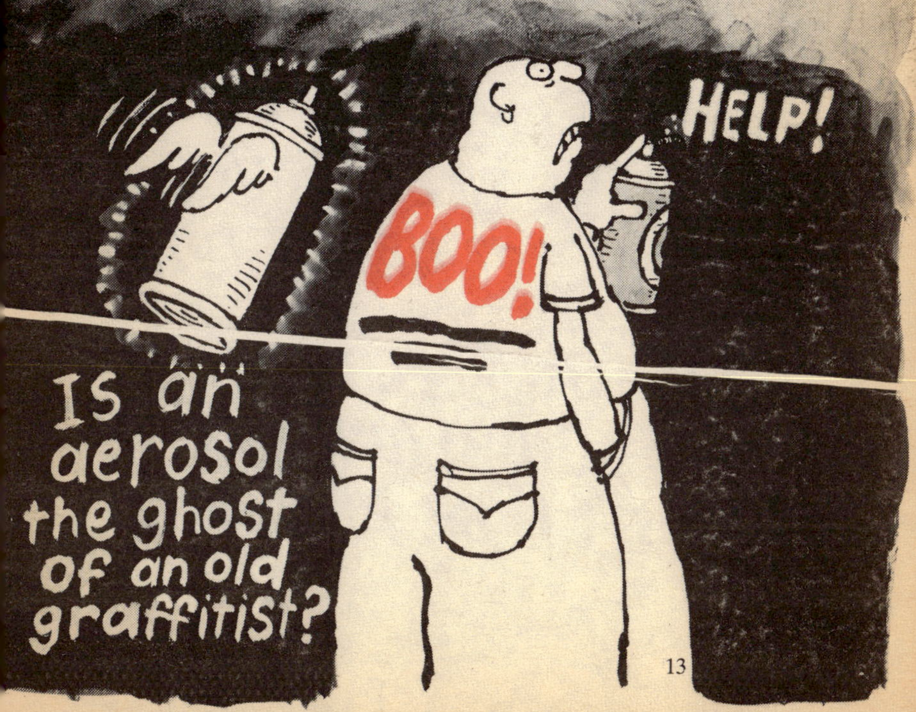

ST JOHN'S SQUARE
I know he is!

Life is like an ashtray – full of little doubts.

KEEP MUSIC LIVE!
– KILL THE PRODUCER
OF 'TOP OF THE POPS.'

IF YOU FEEL BROWNED OFF, GO BLACK HOME, YOU'LL BE ALL WHITE!

THINGS ARE MORE LIKE THEY USED TO BE THAN THEY ARE NOW!

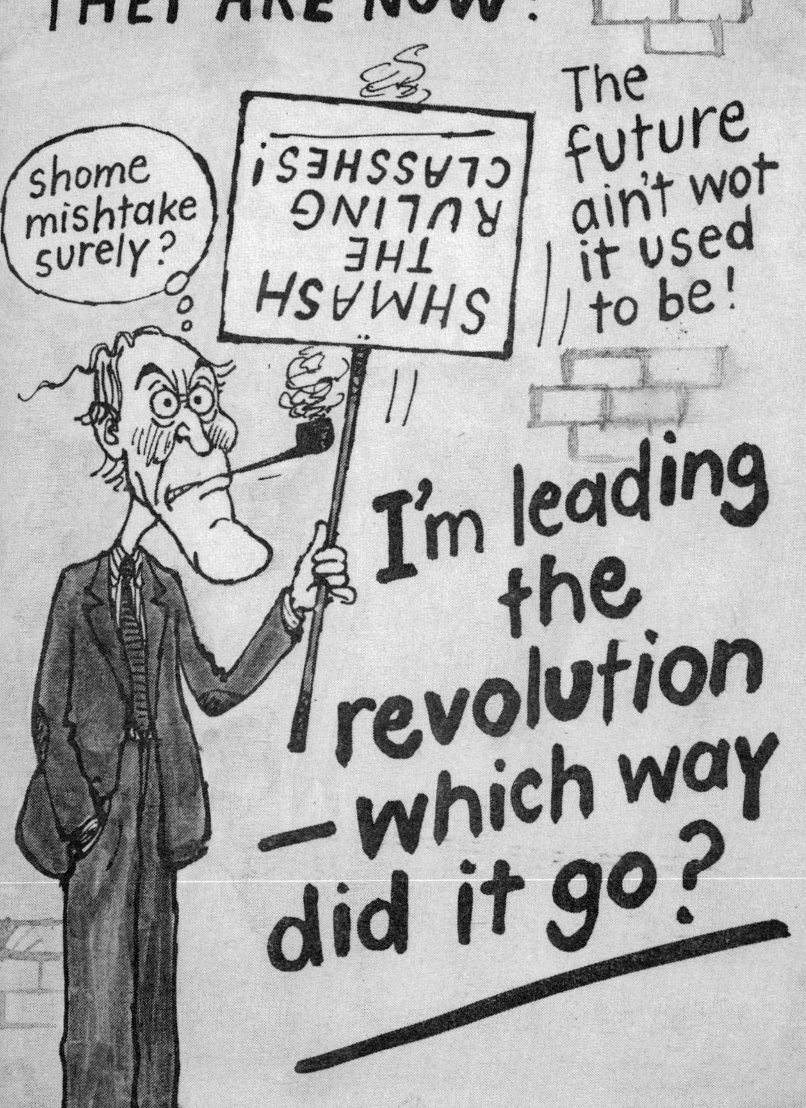

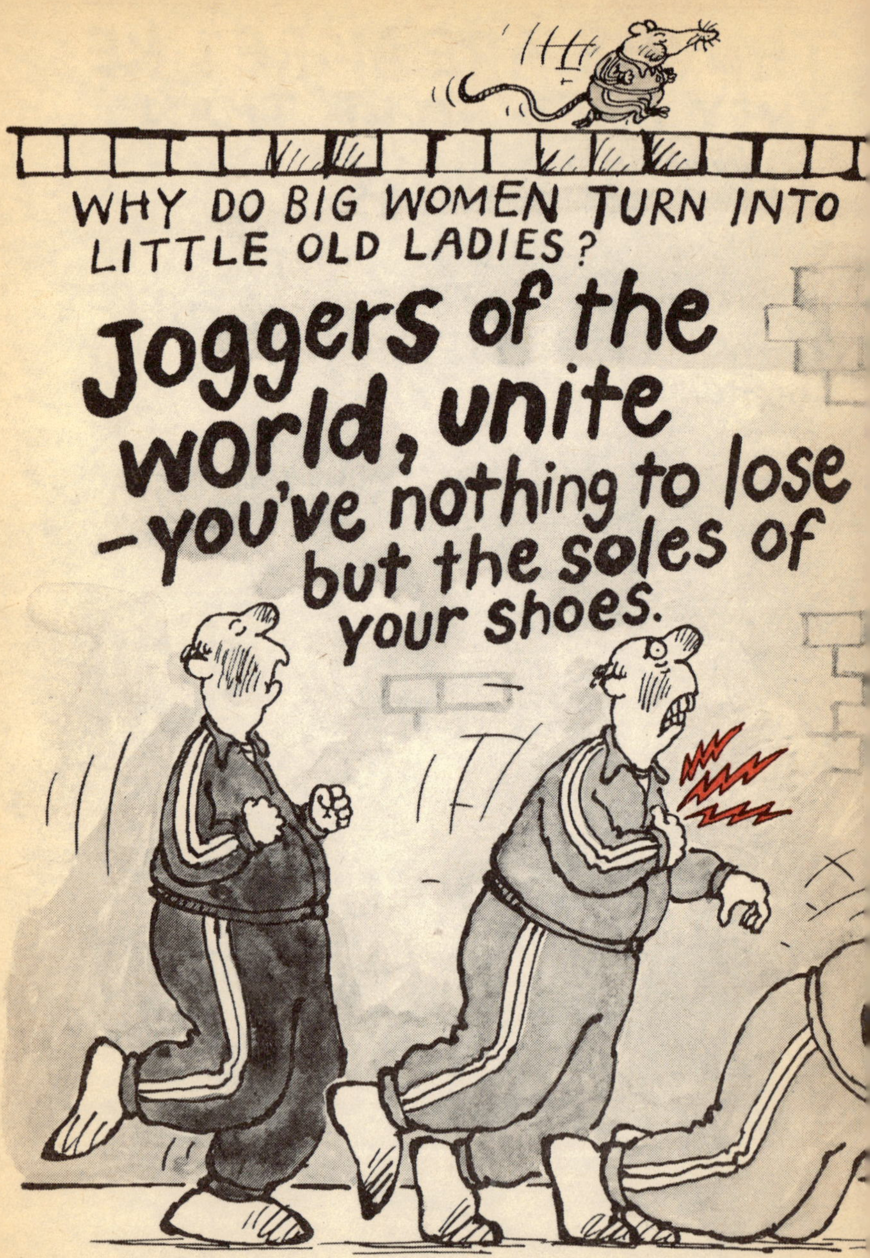

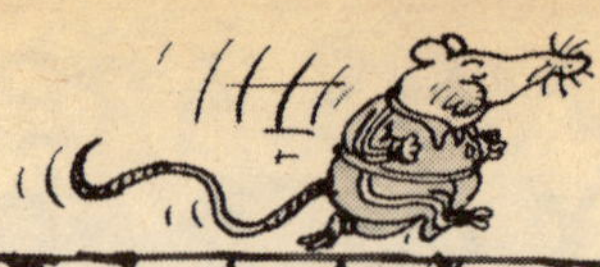

WHY DO BIG WOMEN TURN INTO LITTLE OLD LADIES?

Joggers of the world, unite – you've nothing to lose but the soles of your shoes.

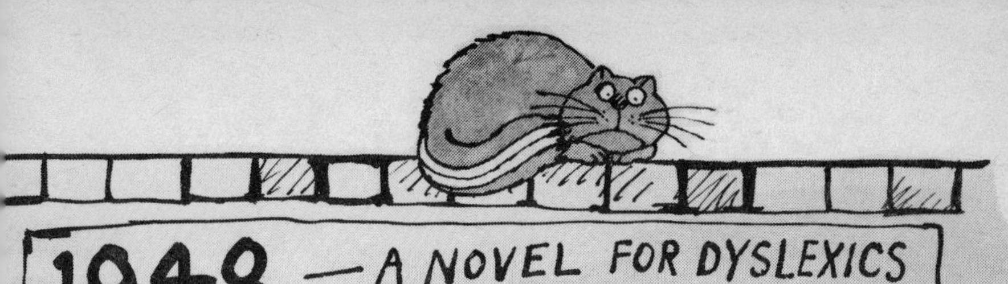
1948 — A NOVEL FOR DYSLEXICS BY GEORGE ORWELL.
Steve McGarret rules — Hawaii 50K
CONSIDERATION RULES — IS THAT OK?

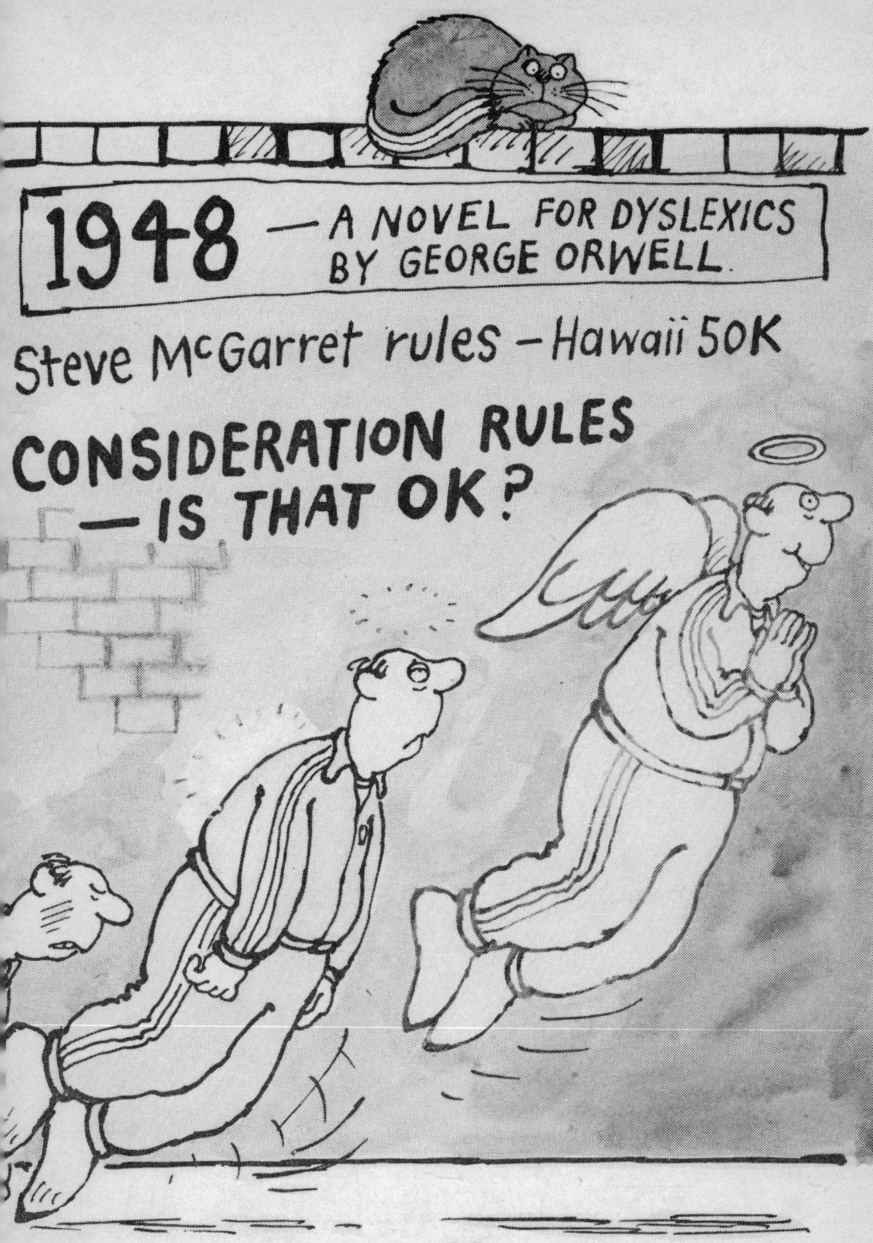

UNEMPLOYMENT IS A GROWTH INDUSTRY

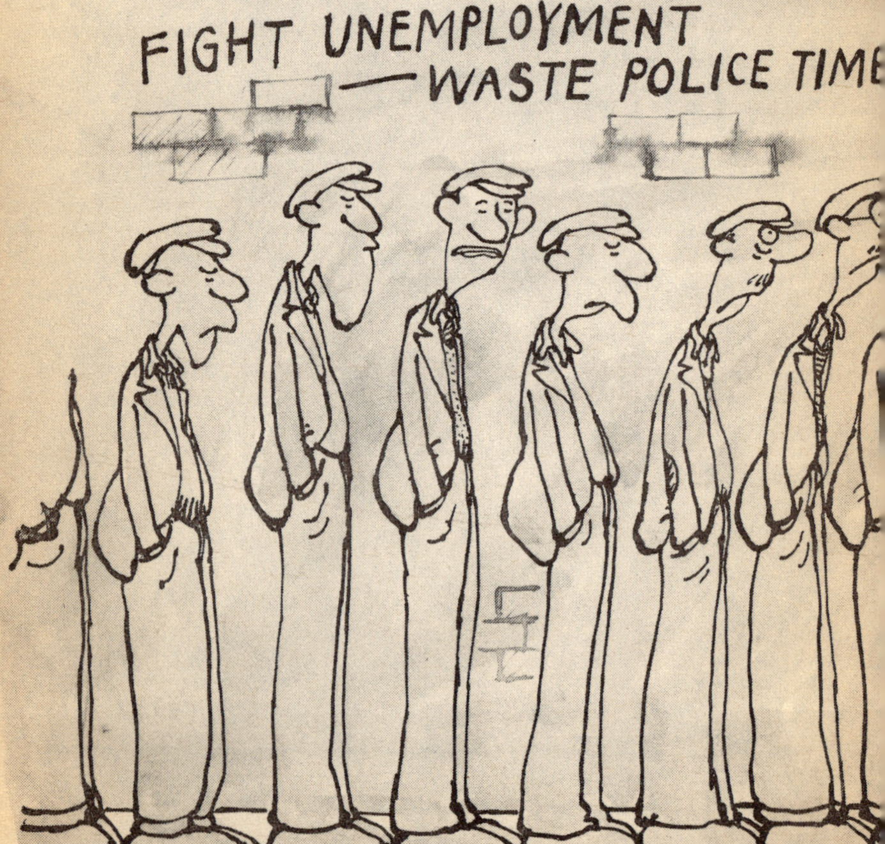

Everything was different before it changed.

MY DOCTOR SAYS I'M SCHIZOPHRENIC BUT I DON'T BELIEVE HIM AND NEITHER DO I.

Don't try and keep up with the Joneses —Jones is on the dole as well!

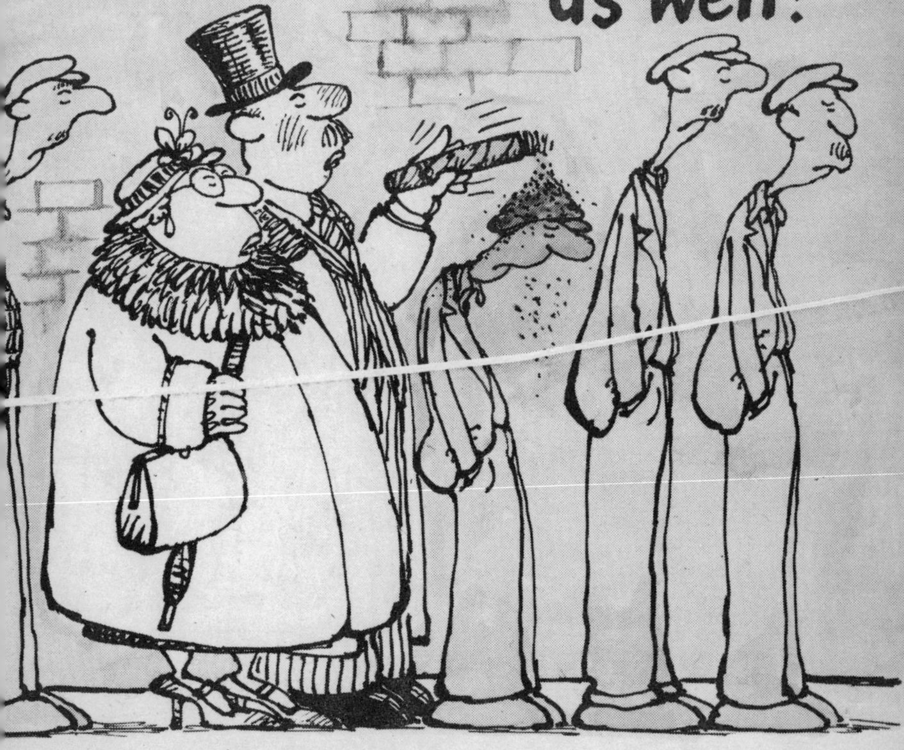

YOU'RE ONLY YOUNG ONCE
-IT'S ALL SOCIETY CAN STAND!

Be different – Get a job!

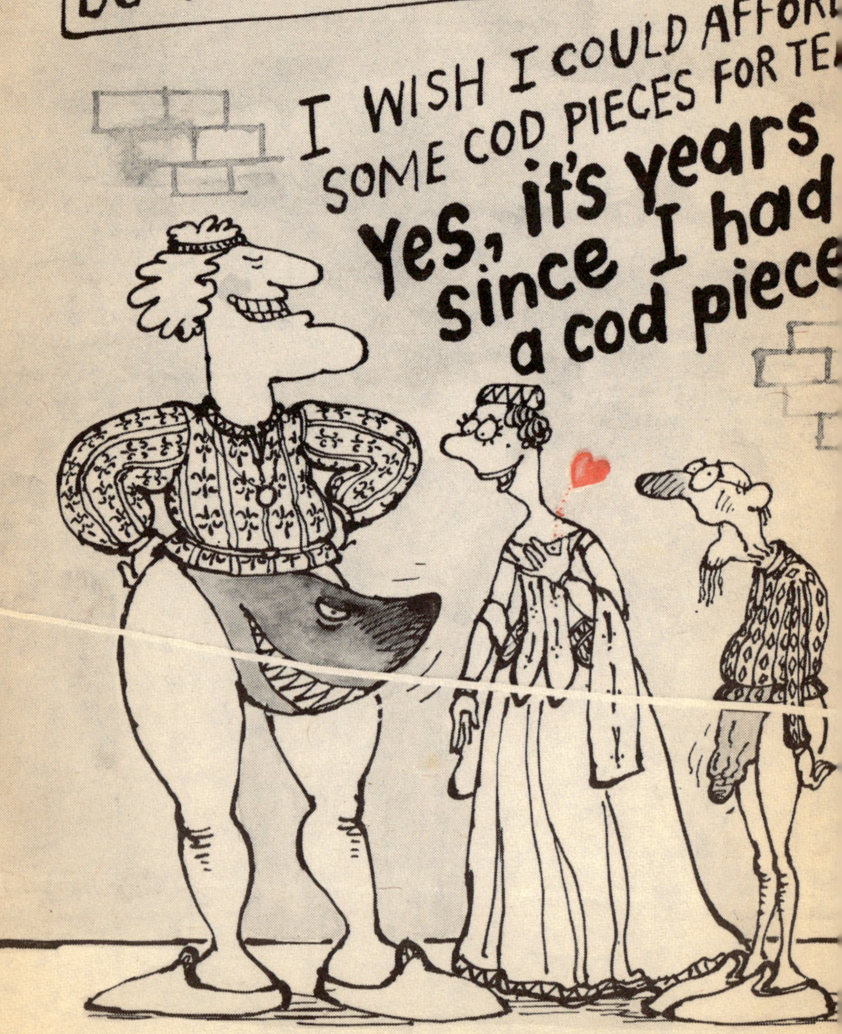

I don't care about apathy

What does apathy mean?

I CAN'T BE BOTHERED TO FIND OUT

APATHY RULES - OH DEAR

What's Lulu's last name?

WHO'S LULU?

SHE'S A LAVATORY ATTENDANT.

FIGHT AGAINST VIOLENCE!

HOW DID THEY SEPARATE THE MEN FROM THE BOYS ON THE OLD SAILING SHIPS? —WITH A CROWBAR!

GRAFFITI IS THE REVENGE OF THE INARTICULATE PROLETARIATE!

When I'm right, nobody remembers. When I'm wrong nobody forgets!

GIVE BARBERS FRINGE BENEFITS!

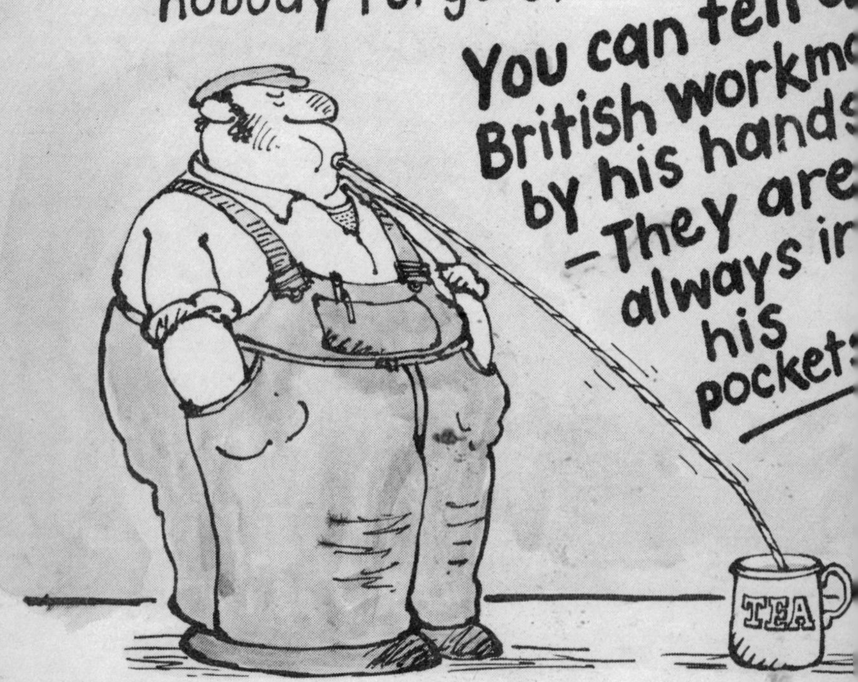

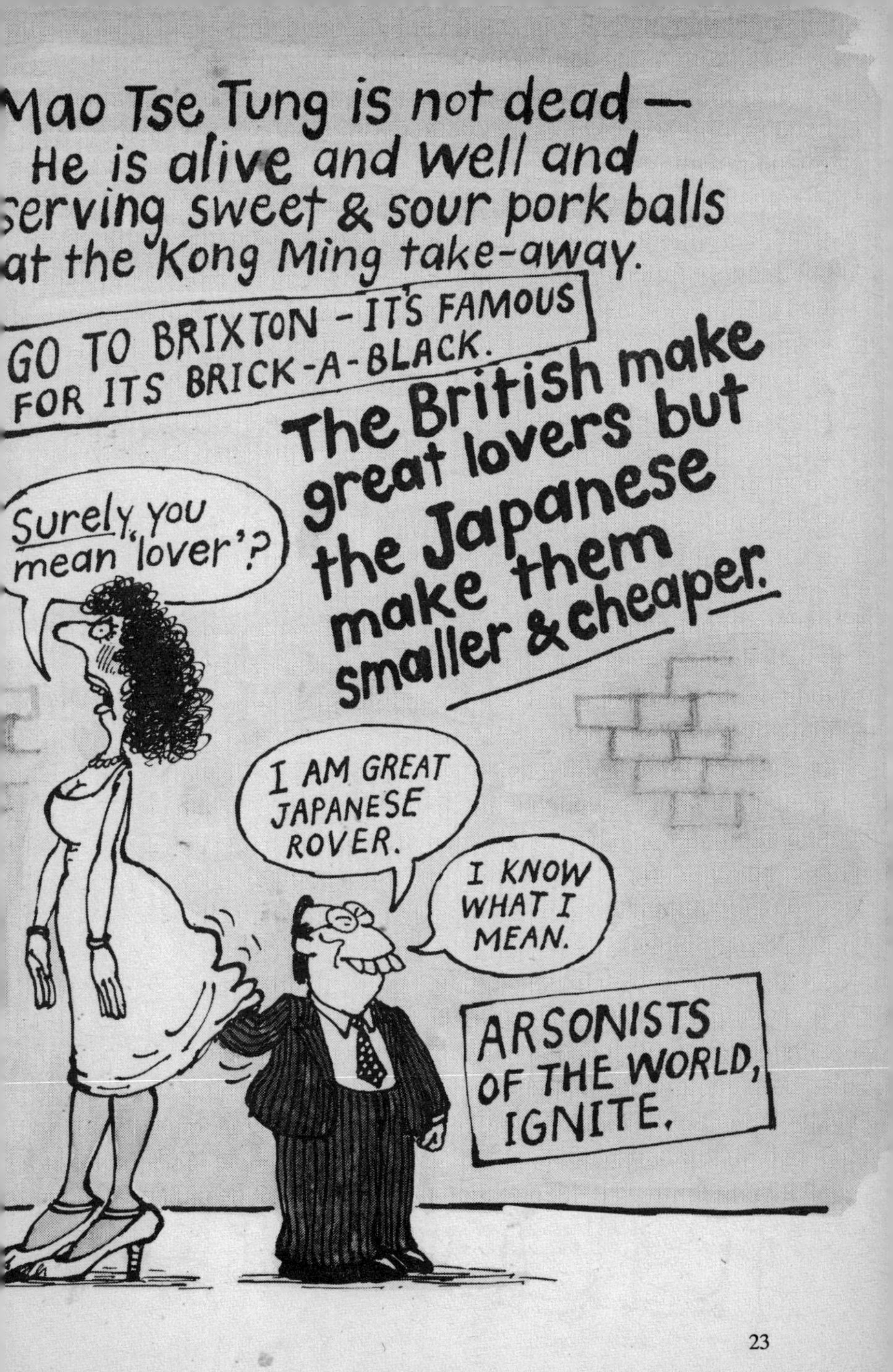

Mao Tse Tung is not dead — He is alive and well and serving sweet & sour pork balls at the Kong Ming take-away.

GO TO BRIXTON - IT'S FAMOUS FOR ITS BRICK-A-BLACK.

The British make great lovers but the Japanese make them smaller & cheaper.

Surely you mean 'lover'?

I AM GREAT JAPANESE ROVER.

I KNOW WHAT I MEAN.

ARSONISTS OF THE WORLD, IGNITE.

MONEY ISN'T EVERYTHING
It isn't even enough!

Scream for Peace!!
– THE GREENHAM COMMON WOME

SKINHEADS HAVE MORE HAIR
THAN BRAINS

If Maggie Thatcher
were dead, I'd jump u
and down on her grave.
I WOULDN'T, I HATE
STANDING IN QUEUES!

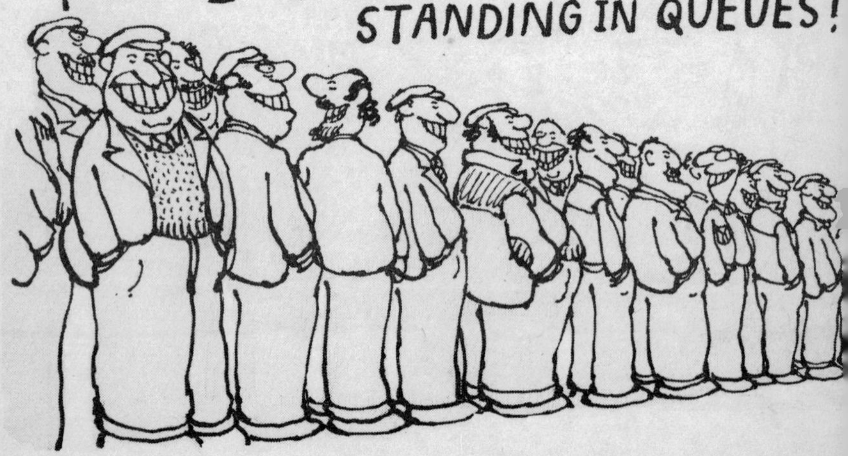

Understanding the Tories unemployment policy is as easy as shaving your eyeballs.

Free the SS20

KILROY IS ONE OF US, UNEMPLOYED AND IN THE SH★THOUSE.

Signed the Gang of 3 Million

Skinhead, skinhead over there
What's it like to have no hair?
Is it warm or is it cold,
Do please tell us 'cos we're not bald.

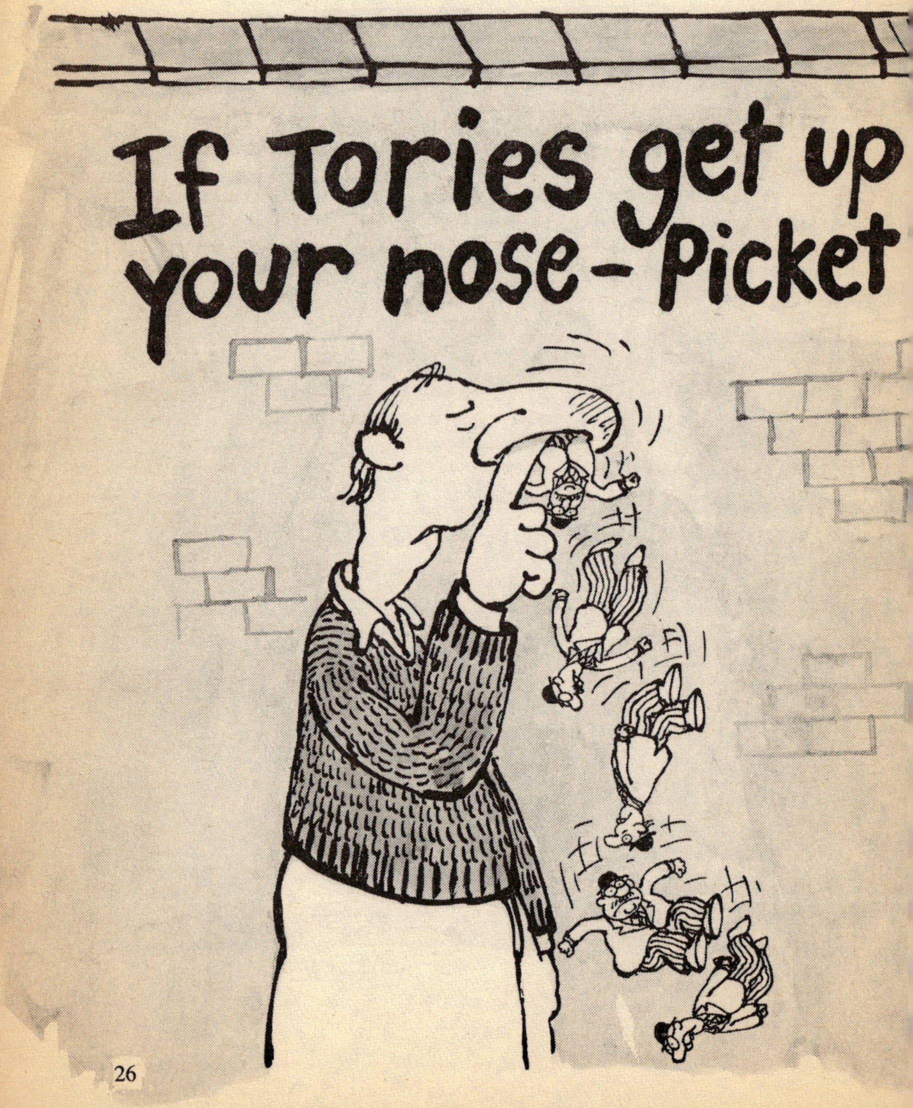

If Tories get up your nose - Picket

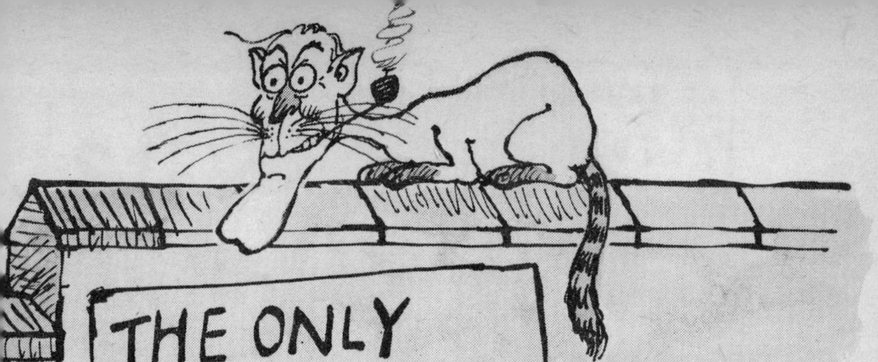

THE ONLY
GOOD TORY
IS A LAVATORY!

I'M CYRIL
SMITH
—FLY ME.

Make your M.P. work
— Don't re-elect him!

ARTHUR
SCARGILL
IS THE PITS

SCOTLAND
RULES
—OK THE
NOO?

Bring back the
BIRCH!

OOH YES PLEASE!!

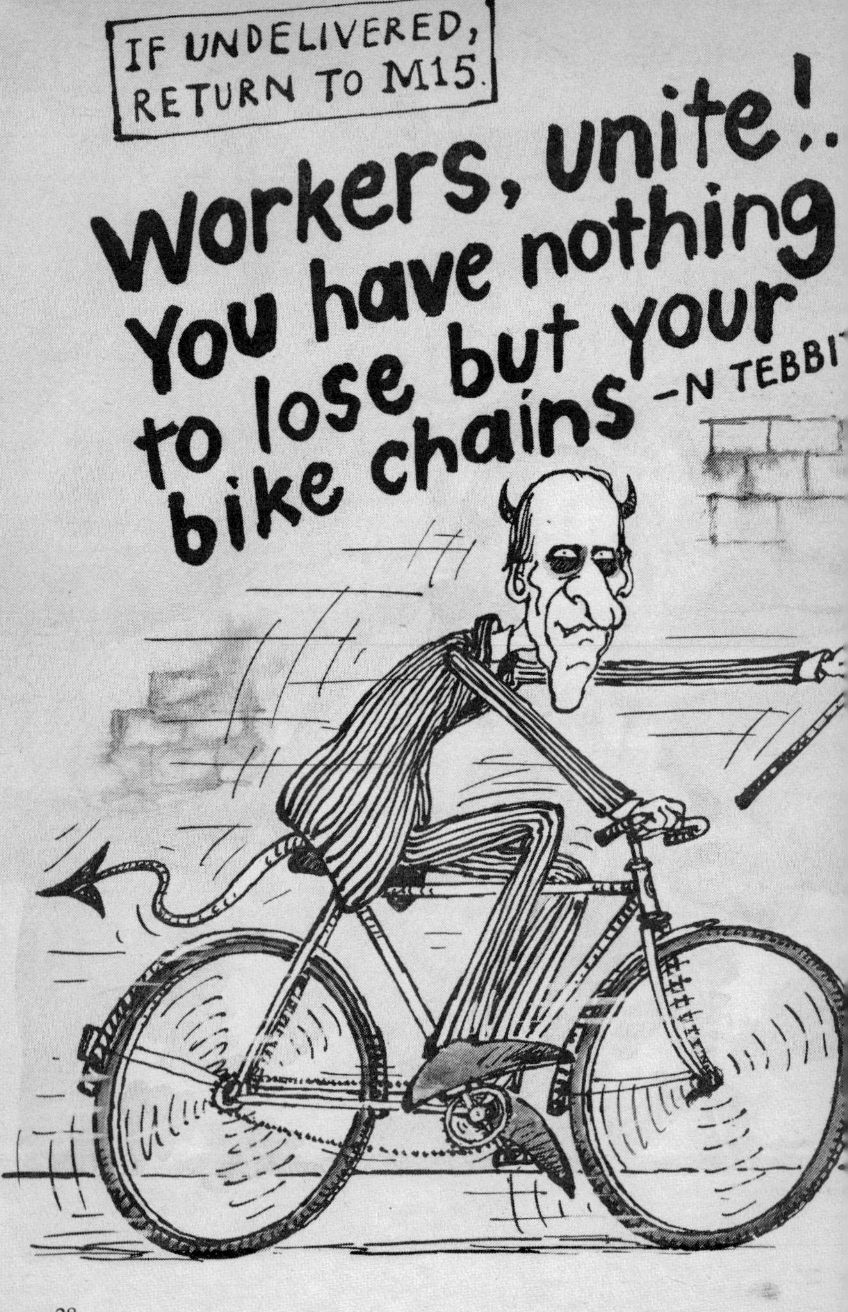

IF UNDELIVERED,
RETURN TO M15.

Workers, unite!..
You have nothing
to lose but your
bike chains -N TEBBI

I'VE HALF A MIND TO JOIN THE S.D.P.

That's all you need!

HELP FIGHT FOOT AND BENN DISEASE!

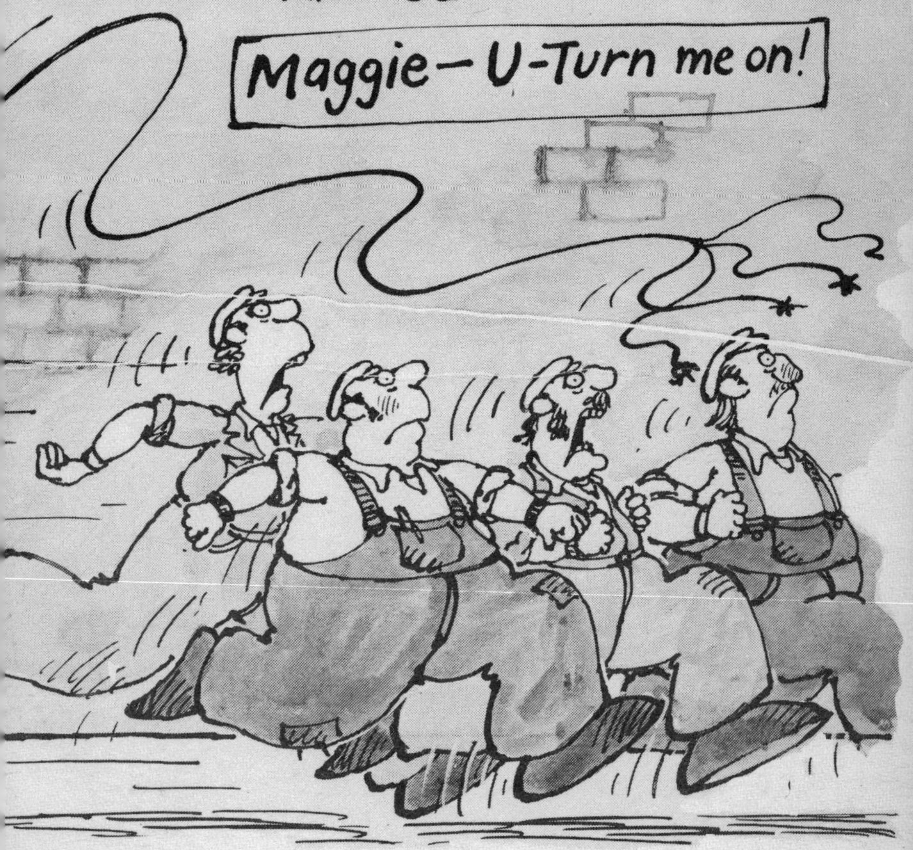

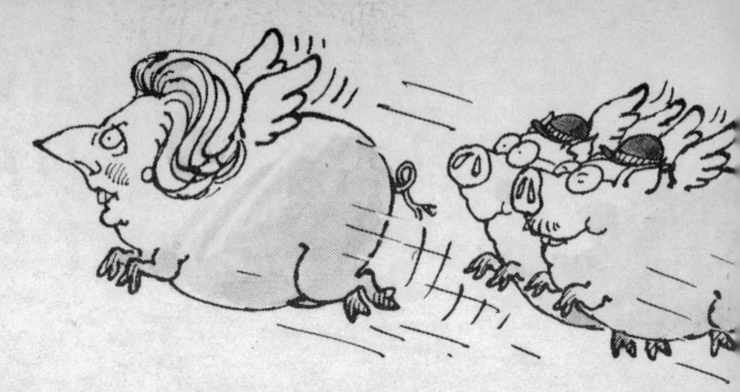

If pigs could fly, I'd make the PM Squadron Leader

1 MILLION DAYS = 2740 YEARS
1 MILLION HOURS = 114 YEARS
1 MILLION MINUTES = 2 YEARS
1 MILLION UNEMPLOYED
= AN IMPOSSIBLE TORY DREA

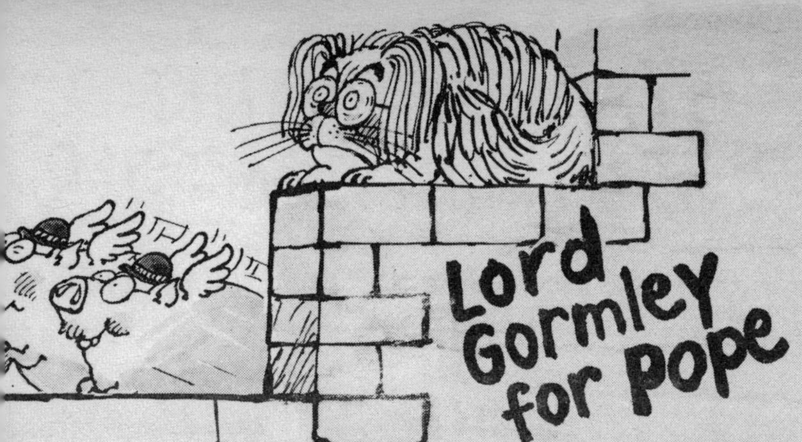

VOTE FOR GUY FAWKES — THE ONLY MAN TO ENTER PARLIAMENT WITH HONEST INTENTIONS!

Is Heseltine a social disease?

NO, HESELTINE IS A MALTY BEDTIME DRINK!

S.D.P. is the answer!

IF S.D.P. IS THE ANSWER, IT MUST BE A BLOODY SILLY QUESTION!

SEND TONY BENN ON A CRUISE..... MISSILE.

Is there life after Tony Benn?

If Maggie's hair falls out will we have to re-Thatcher?

JOIN THE LABOUR PARTY

Why? Are they falling apart?

YES!

Vote for unilateral withdrawal!

IT'LL SOLVE THE POPULATION PROBLEM!

MICHAEL FOOT VOTED BEST DRESSED MAN — ON MARS!

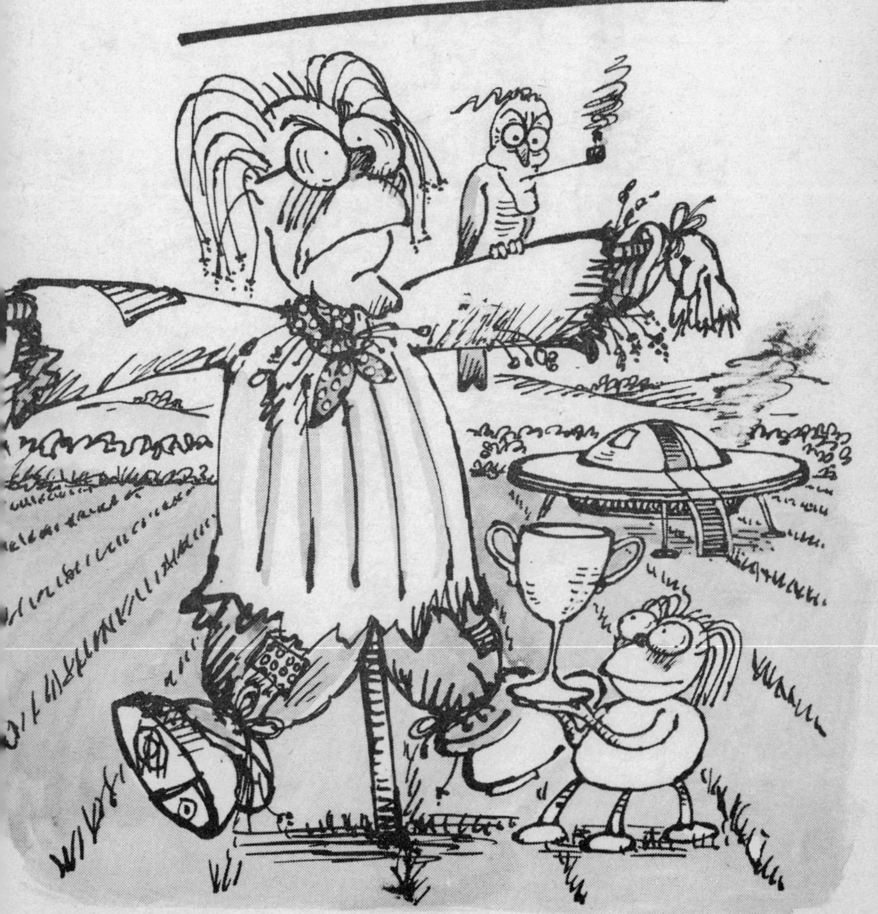

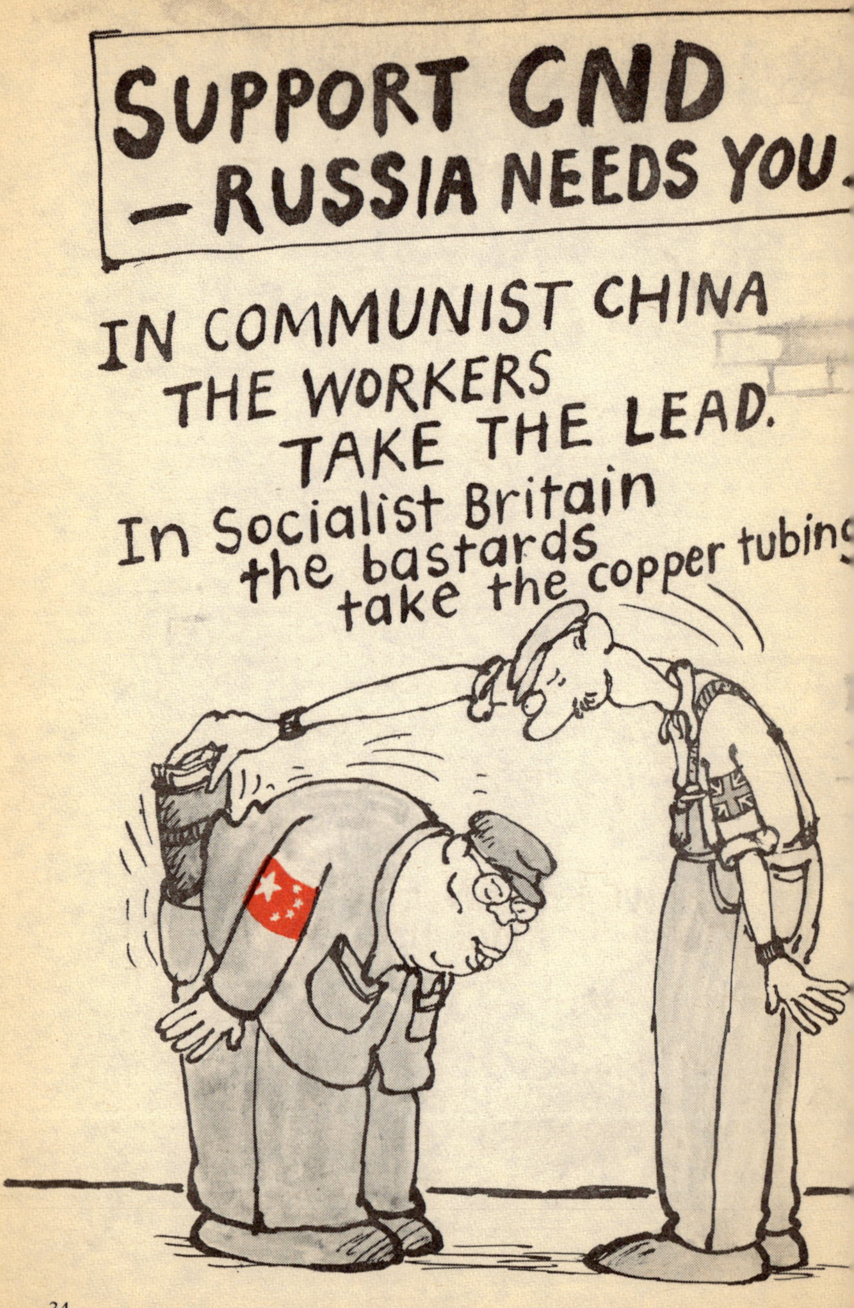

SUPPORT CND
— RUSSIA NEEDS YOU.

IN COMMUNIST CHINA
THE WORKERS
TAKE THE LEAD.
In Socialist Britain
the bastards
take the copper tubing

RONALD REAGAN HAS HAD
SO MANY FACE LIFTS THE
DIMPLE ON HIS CHIN
IS HIS BELLY BUTTON.

**I bet he daren't take
his shirt off!**

If the dimple on his chin
is his belly button,
is that really his tie?

& <u>WHO</u> KNOTS IT?

WHEN WE HAD AN EMPEROR
WE HAD AN EMPIRE
WHEN WE HAD A KING
WE HAD A KINGDOM
NOW WE HAVE MRS. THATCHER
WE HAVE A COUNTRY.

EDUCATION HAS SO MUCH TO LEARN

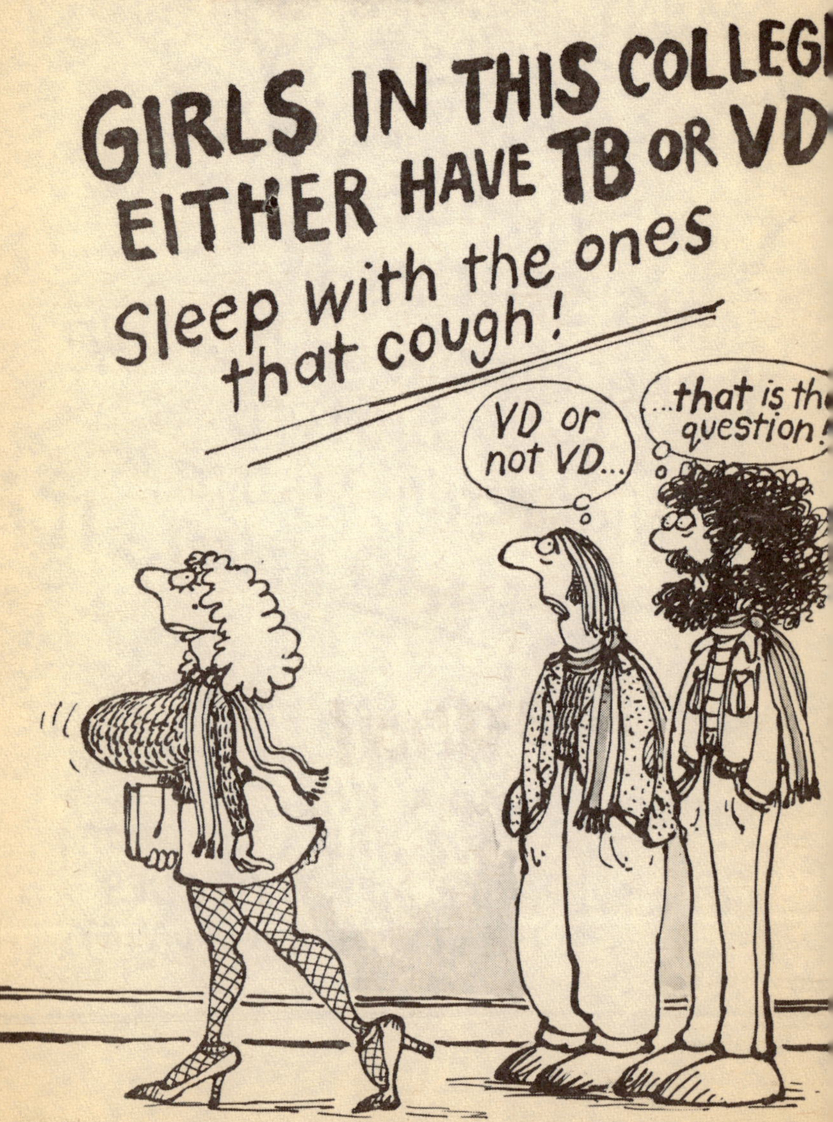

Old professors never die —they just lose their faculties

What is the difference between God and Professor Bonck? God is here but everywhere —Professor Bonck is everywhere but here.

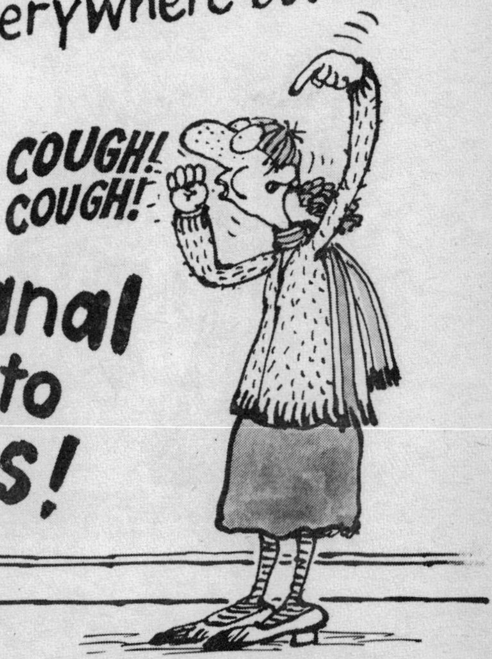

COUGH! COUGH!

Put the anal back into analysis!

Nuclear waste fades your genes.

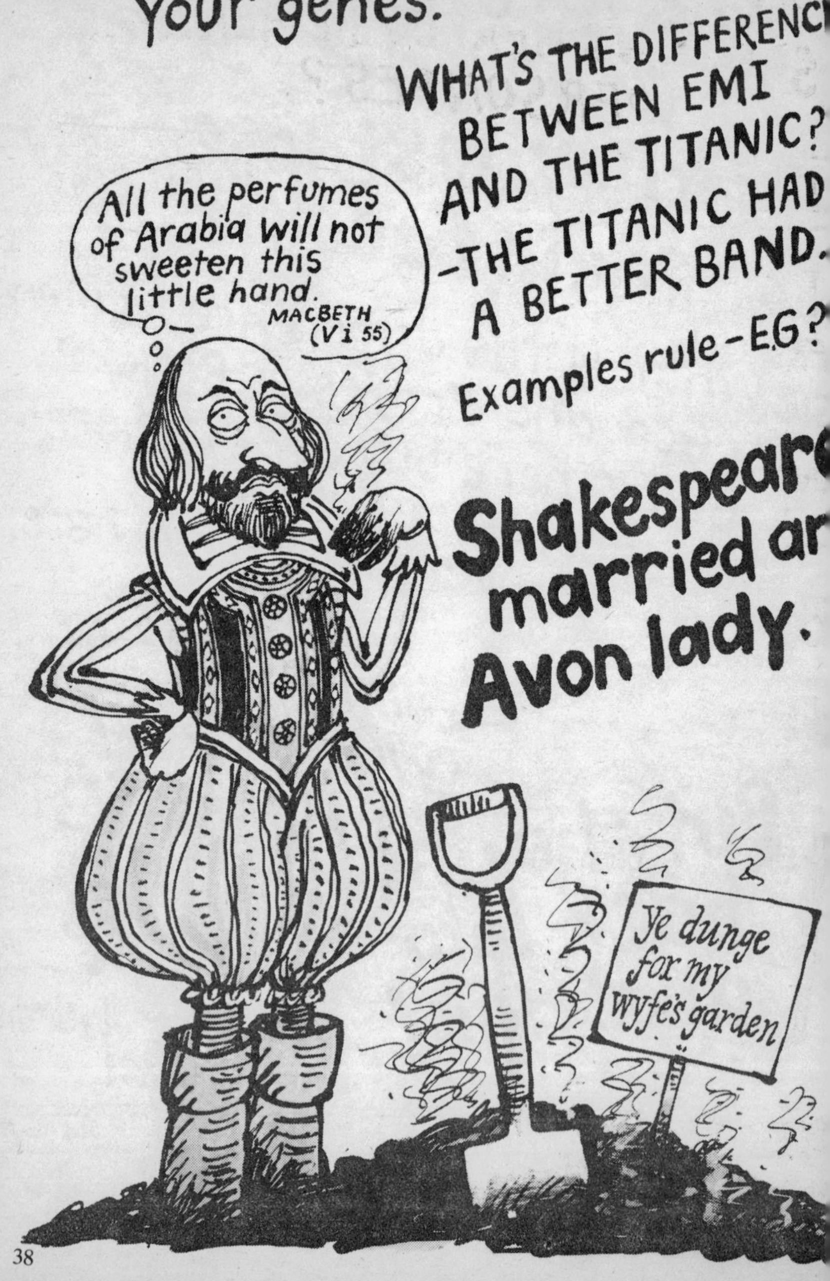

IN THESE DAYS OF EQUALITY SHOULDN'T HERPES BE RENAMED PERSONPES?

I speak Esperanto like a native.

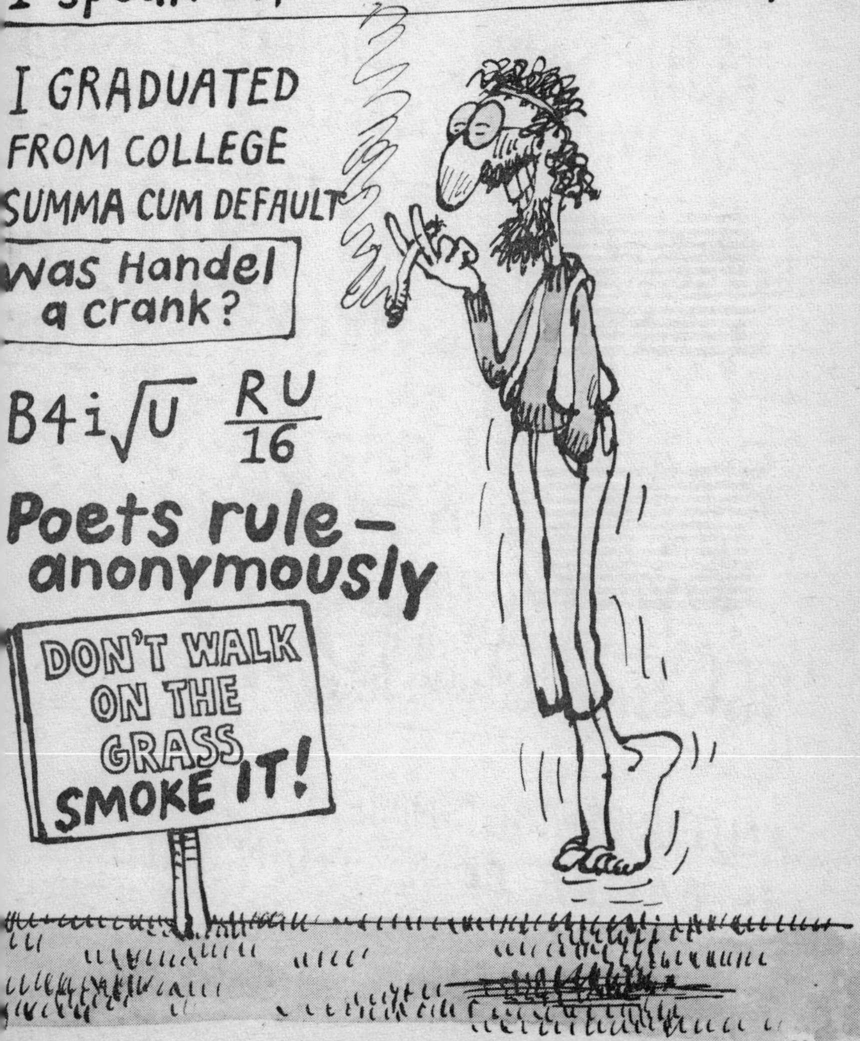

Psychology is getting habits out of rats.

PHILOSOPHY : UNINTELLIGIBLE ANSWERS TO INSOLUBLE PROBLEMS

MARIJUANA — NATURE'S WAY OF SAYING 'HIGH'.

Study Art and Logic — and learn to draw your own conclusions

Potassium ethoxide rules C_2H_3OK!

ANTIDISESTABLISHMENTARIANISM IS EASIER DONE THAN SAID.

IQ — Idiot Quotient

DOCTORS ARE MAKING GREAT PROGRESS — WHAT USED TO BE AN ITCH IS NOW AN ALLERGY.

I don't mind going to lectures — It's the long wait to get home I don't like.

Racial prejudice is a pigment of the imagination.

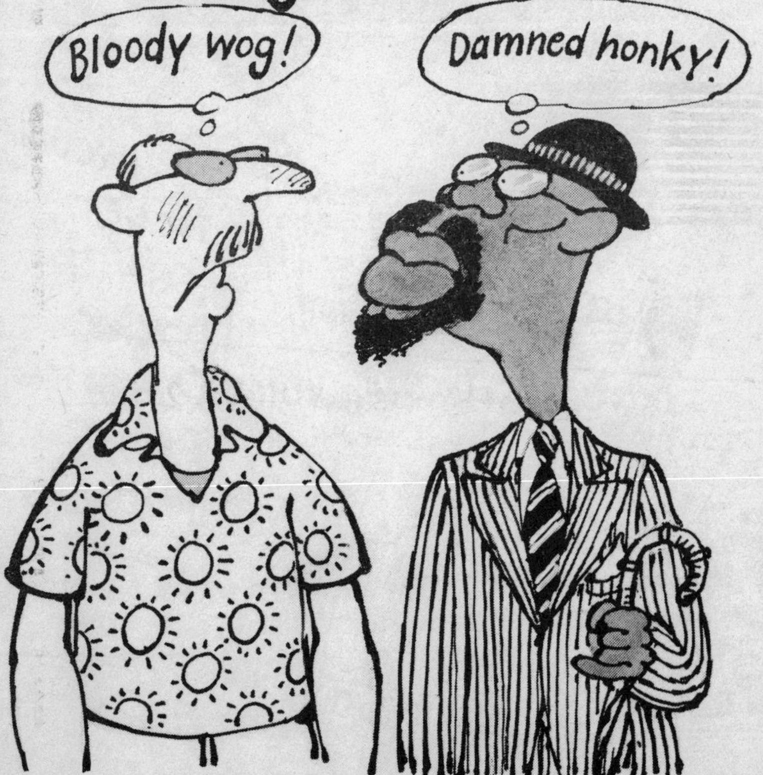

DANCING IS SIMPLY A PERPENDICULAR EXPRESSION OF A HORIZONTAL DESIRE.

H.G. Wells was an optimist

SO WAS GEORGE ORWELL

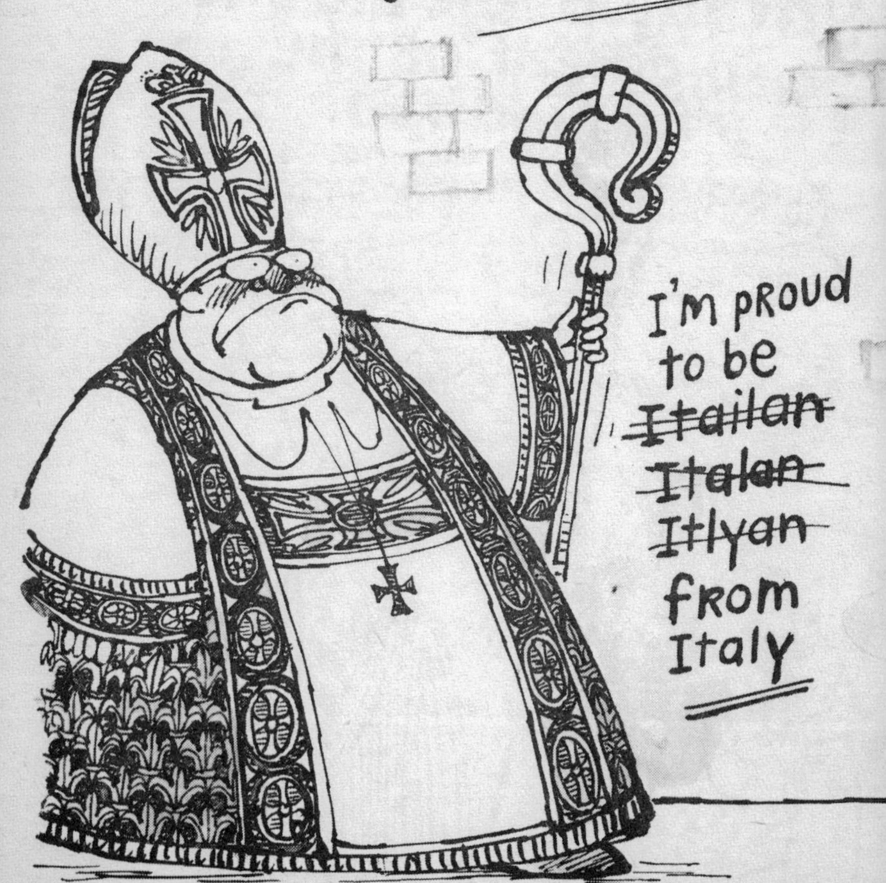

Musicians do it with an instrument.

CARPENTERS DO IT WITH THEIR TOOLS.

Handymen do it with their hands.

Lumberjacks do it with their choppers.

CYCLISTS HAVE IT BETWEEN THEIR LEGS.

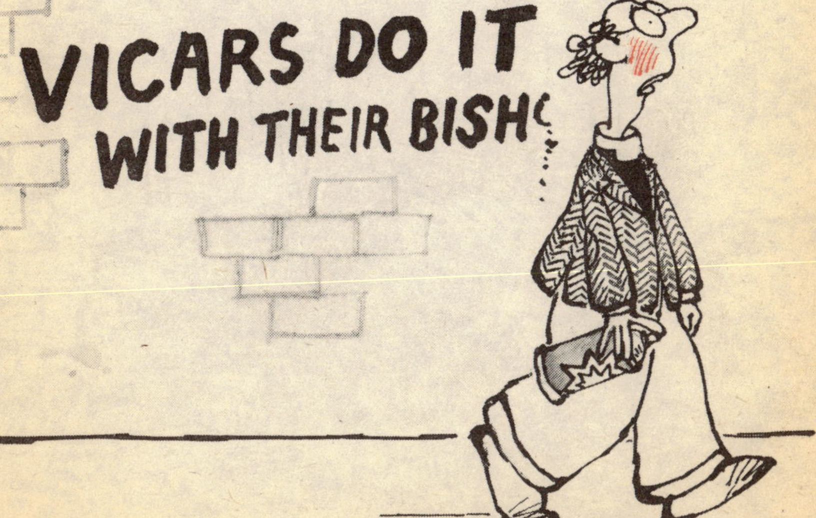

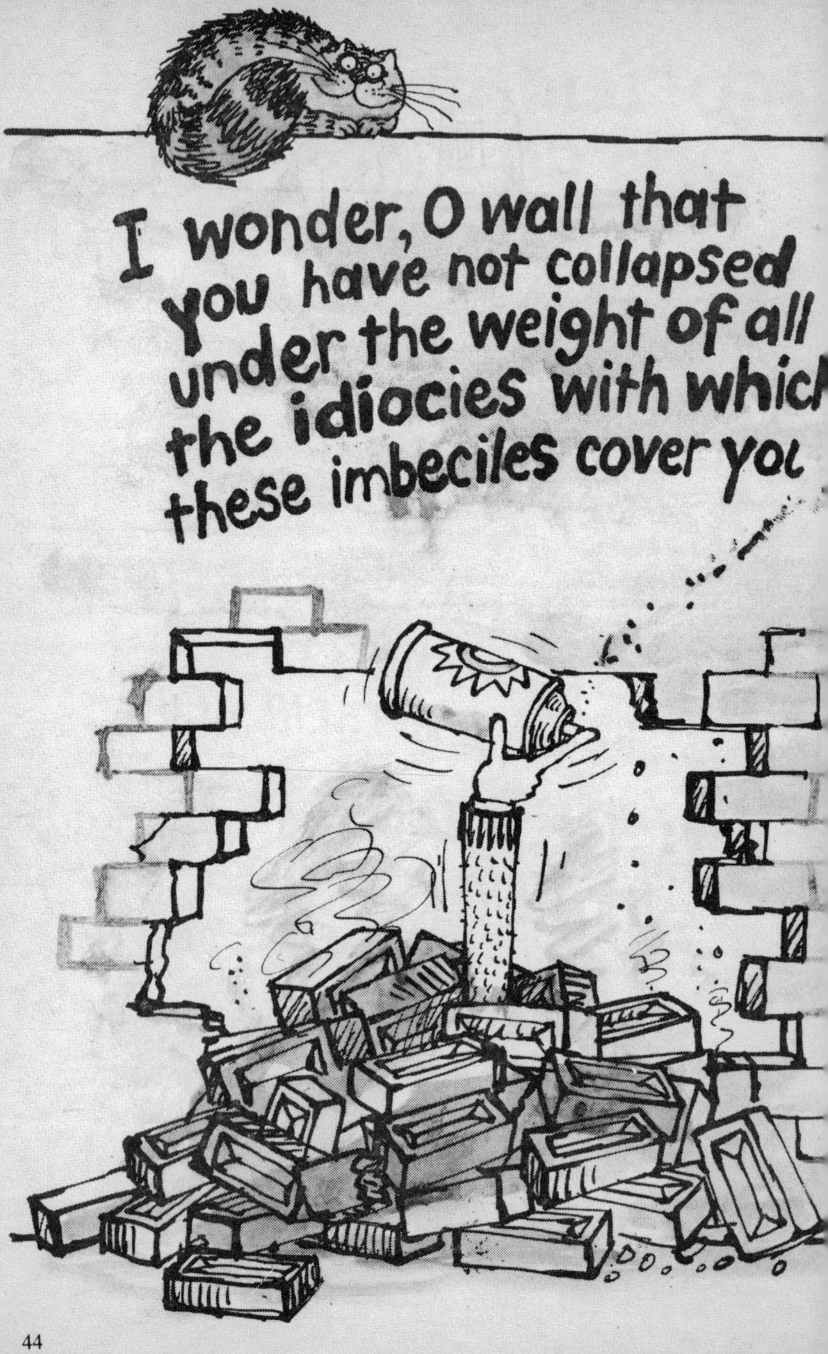

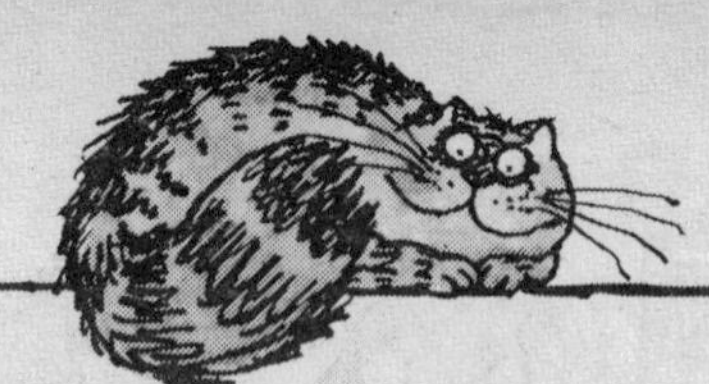
I wonder, O wall that
you have not collapsed
under the weight of all
the idiocies with whic
these imbeciles cover yo

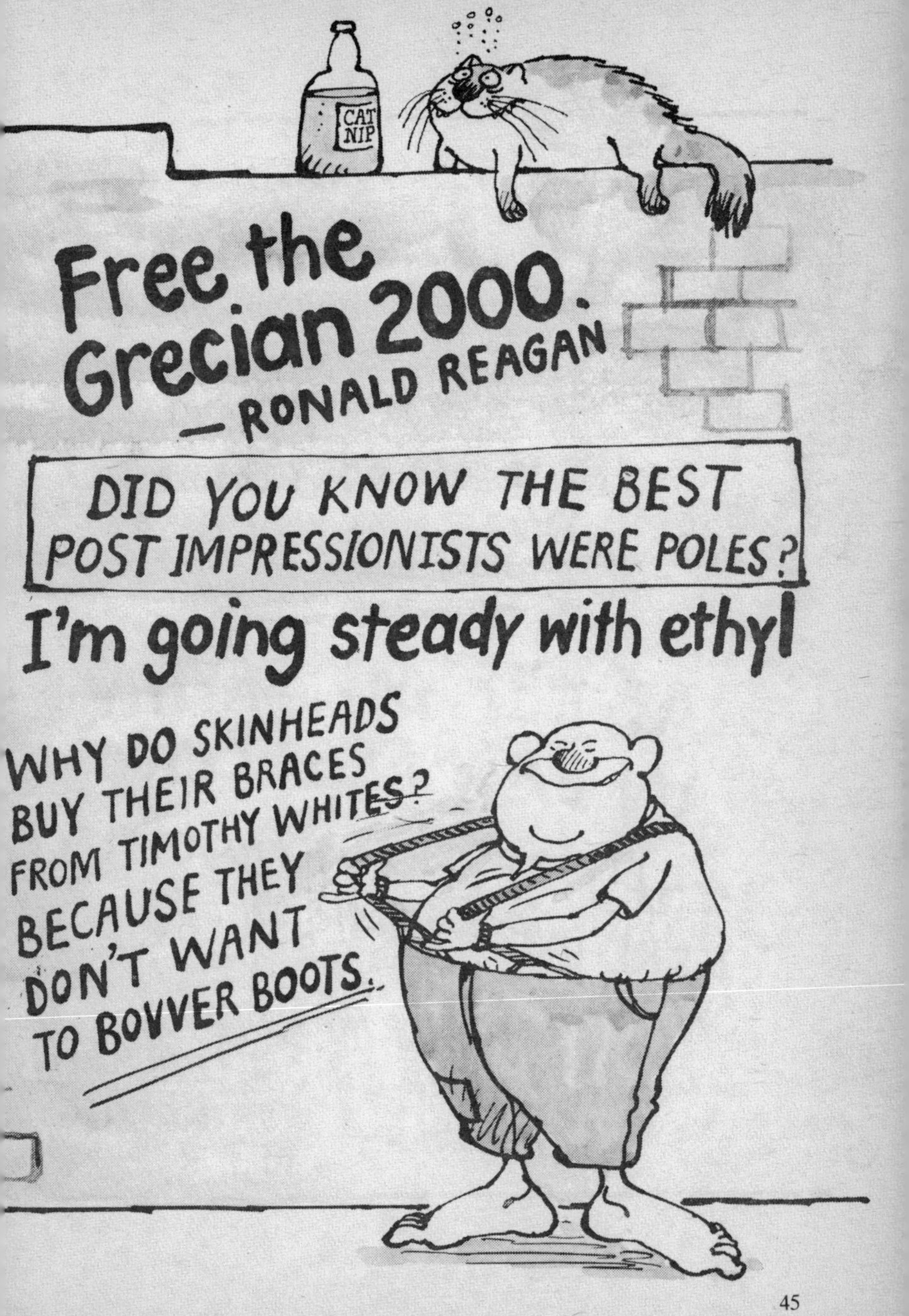

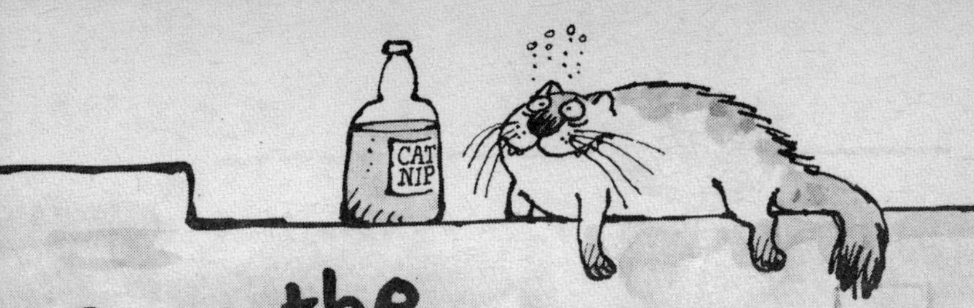

Free the Grecian 2000.
— RONALD REAGAN

DID YOU KNOW THE BEST POST IMPRESSIONISTS WERE POLES?

I'm going steady with ethyl

WHY DO SKINHEADS BUY THEIR BRACES FROM TIMOTHY WHITES? BECAUSE THEY DON'T WANT TO BOVVER BOOTS.

IT TAKES AN AGE FOR ONE TO ARRIVE

This is the age of the train.
OURS WAS 92!

ASLEF MY TRAIN IN SAN FRANCISCO

THE APT TRAIN NOW ARRIVING AT PLATFORM 3 WILL BE STOPPING AT CREWE, WARRINGTON WIGAN, PRESTON, LANCASTER & CARLISLE .... FOR REPAIRS.

IS THIS COCKFOSTERS?

PLATFORM

No, it's mine!

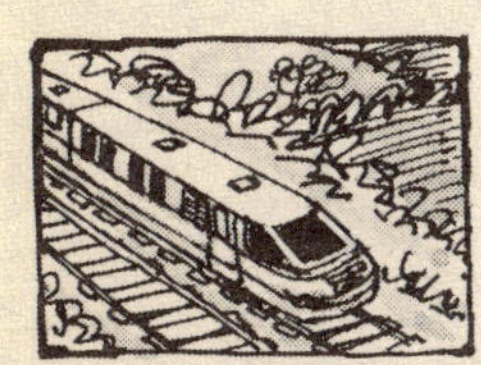

YORK – 2 hrs 5 mins.
SHEFFIELD – 3 hrs 20 mins
EDINBURGH – 4 hrs 12 mi

SOME TRAINS ARE EVEN LATER

Inter-City trains are fully air-conditioned

ONLY BECAUSE THE WINDOWS ARE STUCK!

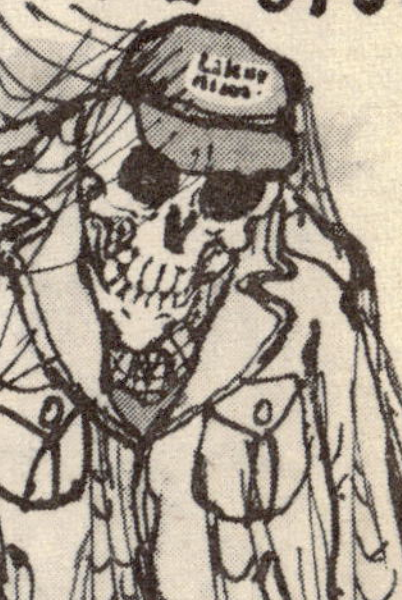

Can Jim fix it for me to nuke Southern Region?

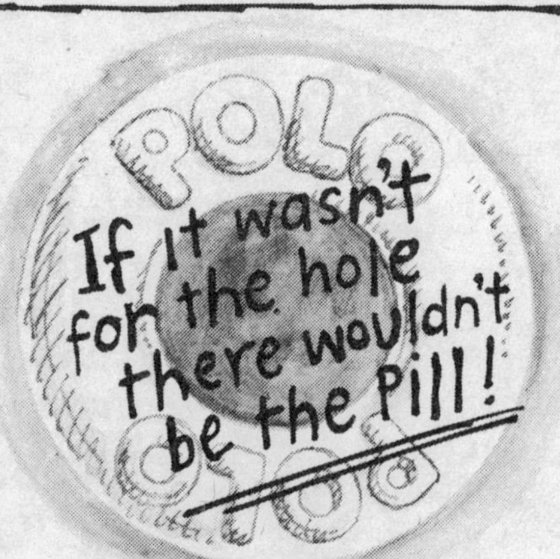

WE WANT MORE FEMALE TRAIN DRIVERS — A WOMAN HAS A RIGHT TO CHOO-CHOOSE

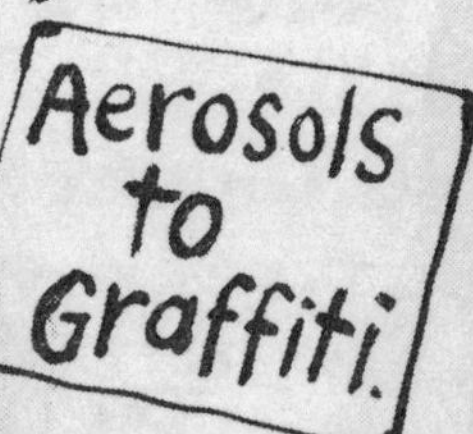

I'd travel by train more often if I wasn't so afraid of meeting Jimmy Savile

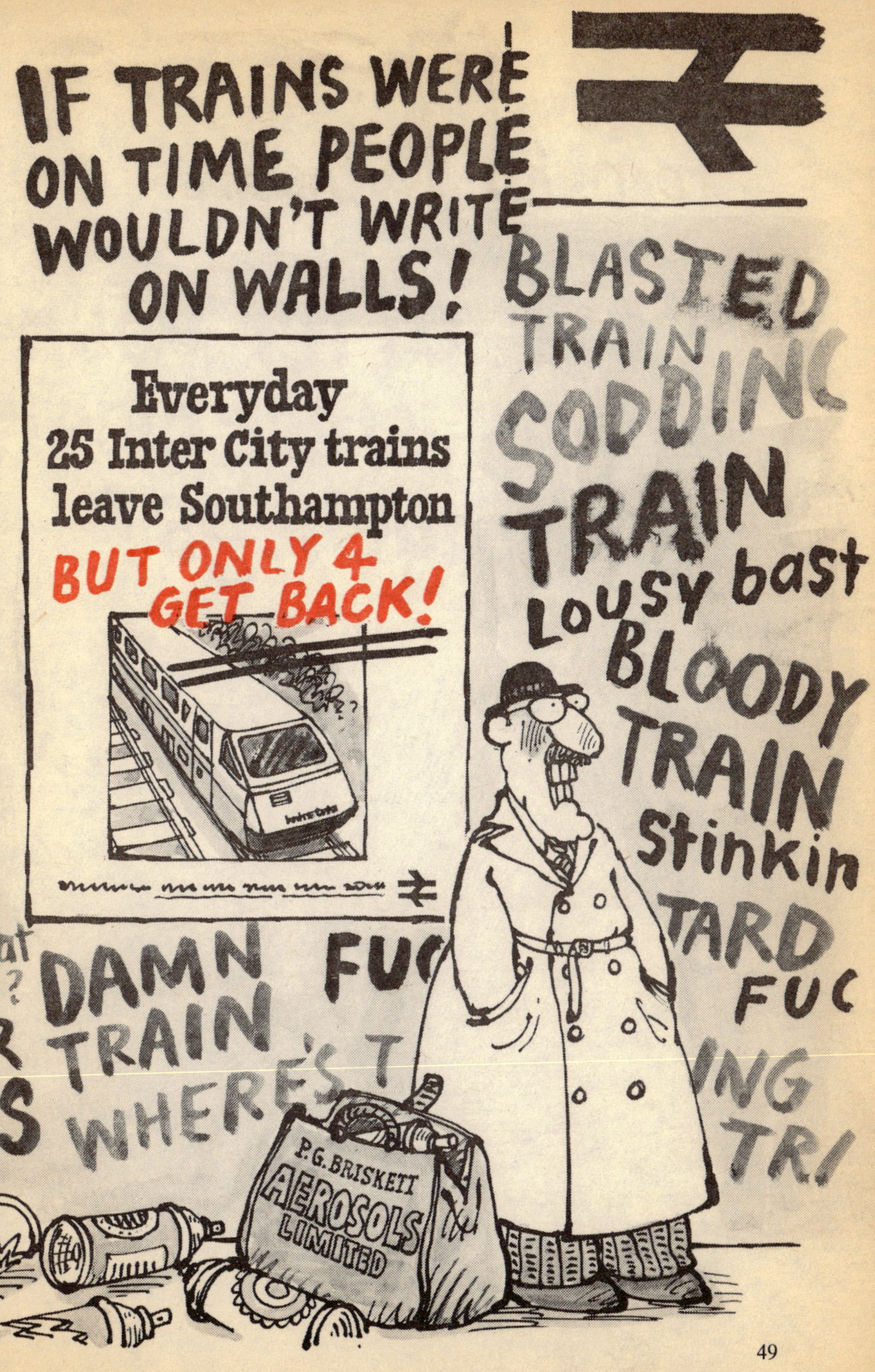
IF TRAINS WERE ON TIME PEOPLE WOULDN'T WRITE ON WALLS!
Everyday
25 Inter City trains
leave Southampton
BUT ONLY 4 GET BACK!
BLASTED
TRAIN
SODDING
TRAIN
LOUSY bast
BLOODY
TRAIN
Stinkin
TARD
FUC
ING
TRI
DAMN
TRAIN
WHERE'S T
FUC
P.G. BRISKETT
AEROSOLS
LIMITED

THERE IS NOTHING LIKE A DAIMLER

Look after your tyres, steer clear of hedgehogs!

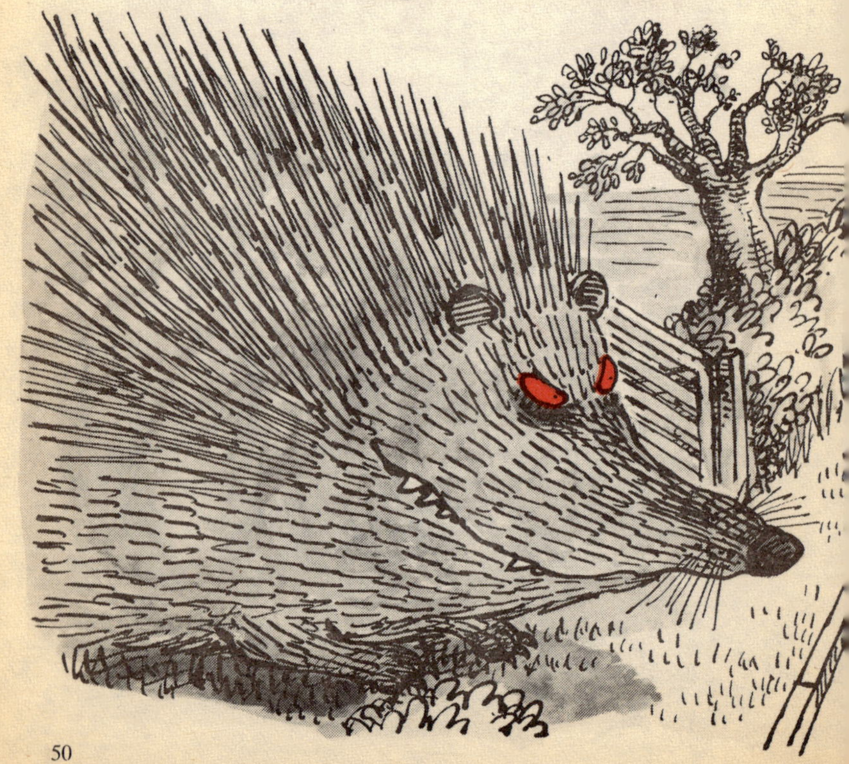

DRIVERS – DON'T PULL OUT TO AVOID A CHILD. You might fall off the bed!

PRESERVE US FROM TRAFFIC JAMS

I'm utterly convinced
Sir Robert Mark needs a re-tread.

IT TAKES A MILLION NUTS
TO BUILD A CAR —
AND ONLY ONE TO WRECK IT!

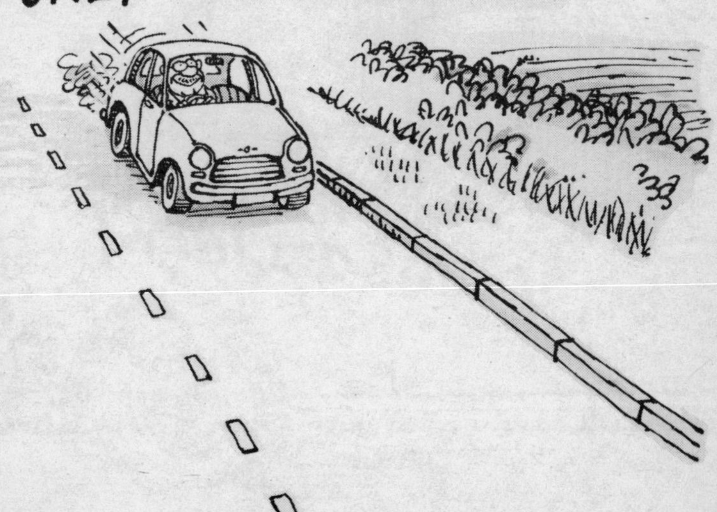

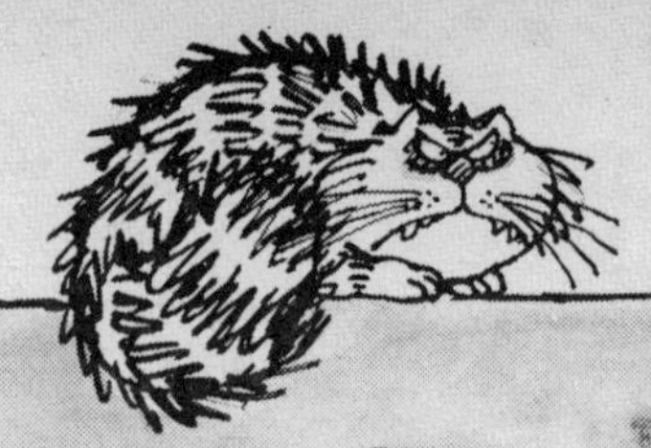

Always carry a bit of spare.

My car has hand operated windows.

MY AUSTIN MÄESTRO ISN'T TALKING TO ME.

Mine lisps!

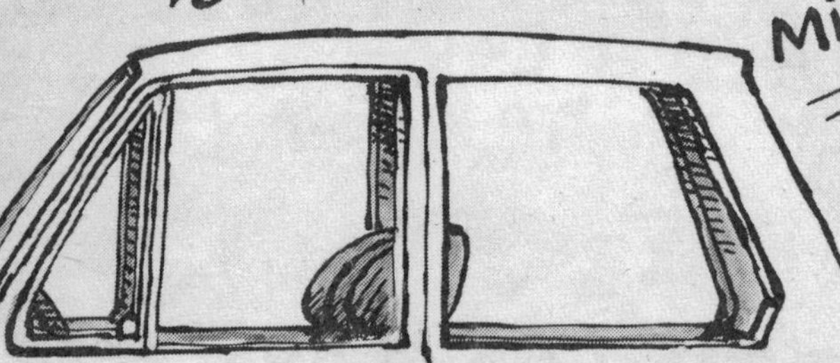

I was a Rolls Royce before the accident.

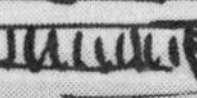

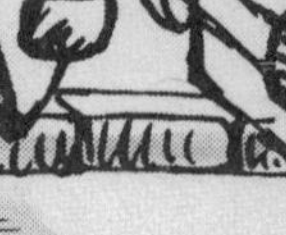

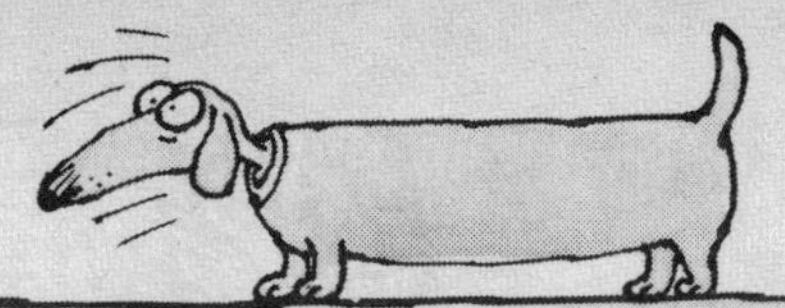

DOWN WITH THE
NODDING DOGS OF
CAPITALISM

They don't make cars
like they auto.

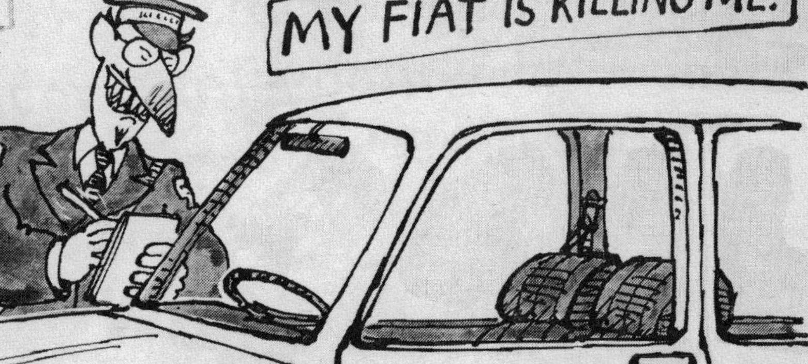

THIS CAR IS RUST FREE
— THE DEALER
DIDN'T CHARGE FOR IT.

DRIVE WITH CARE—
DON'T INSIST ON YOUR RITES

Sex is great in a car—
pull in a labia tonight.

How do you stop a mod from drowning—Take your foot off his head.

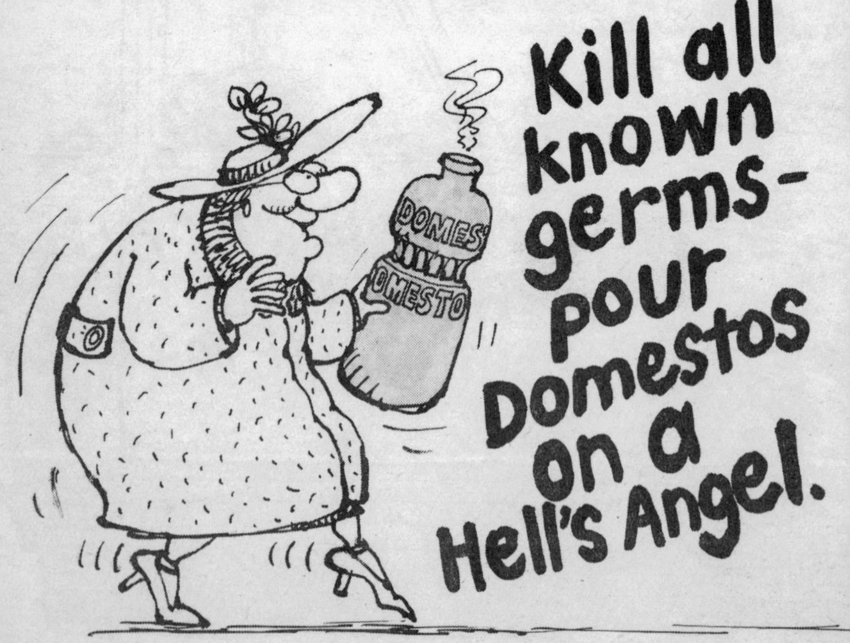

BARBARA WOODHOUSE
DRIVES A SIT-RON

God is dead!

I'M SORRY, OFFICER,
I DIDN'T SEE HIM

CARS CAN DAMAGE YOUR HEALTH.

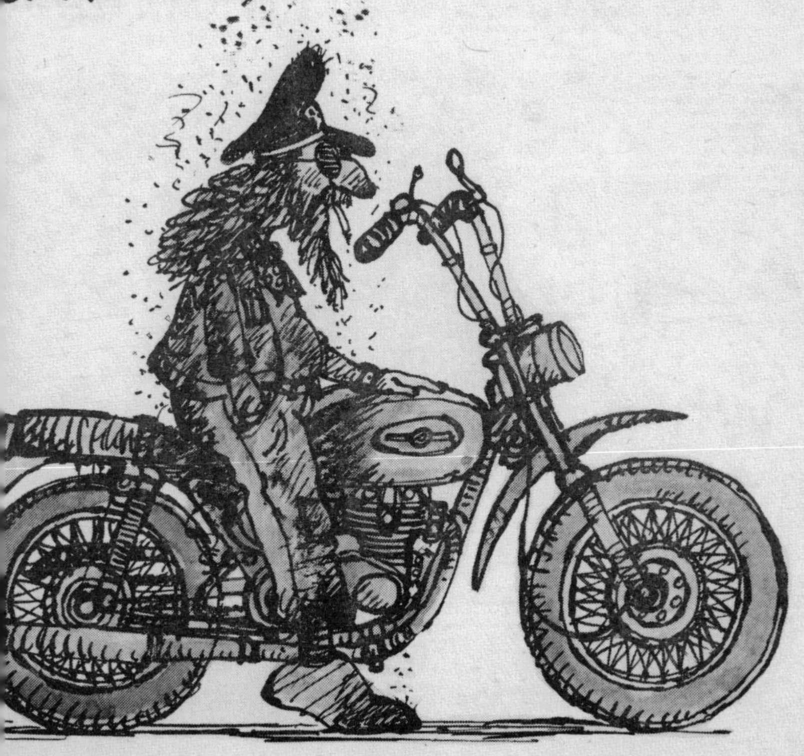

IF A WOMAN WANTS TO LEARN TO DRIVE, DON'T STAND IN HER WAY.

I DRIVE THE HATCHBACK OF NOTRE DAME

Some joy rides extend from here to maternity.

DON'T PLAY IN THE STREET
–YOU MIGHT GET THAT RUN DOWN FEELING

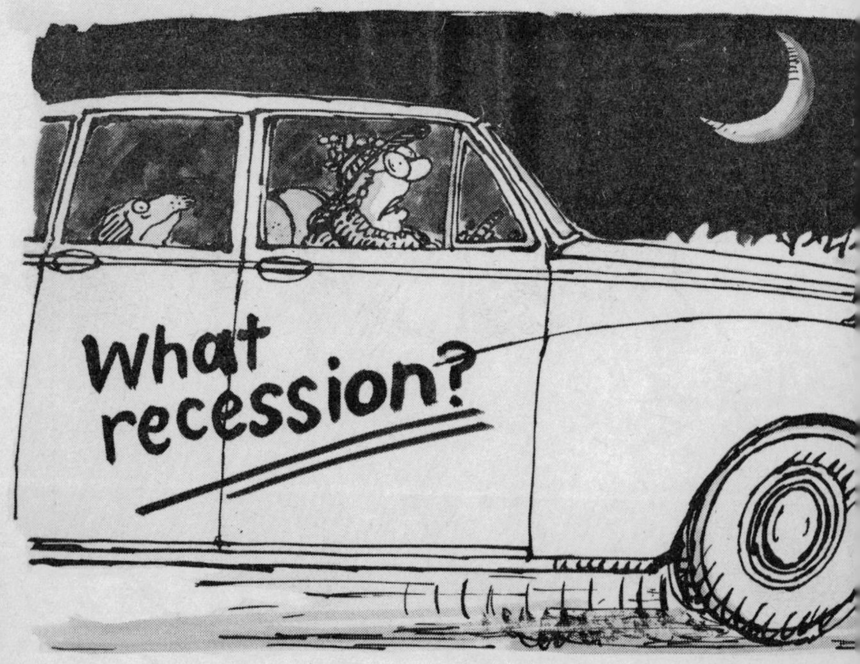

Let's not meet by accident.

LET'S NOT MEET BECAUSE OF ONE

I'm the result of one!

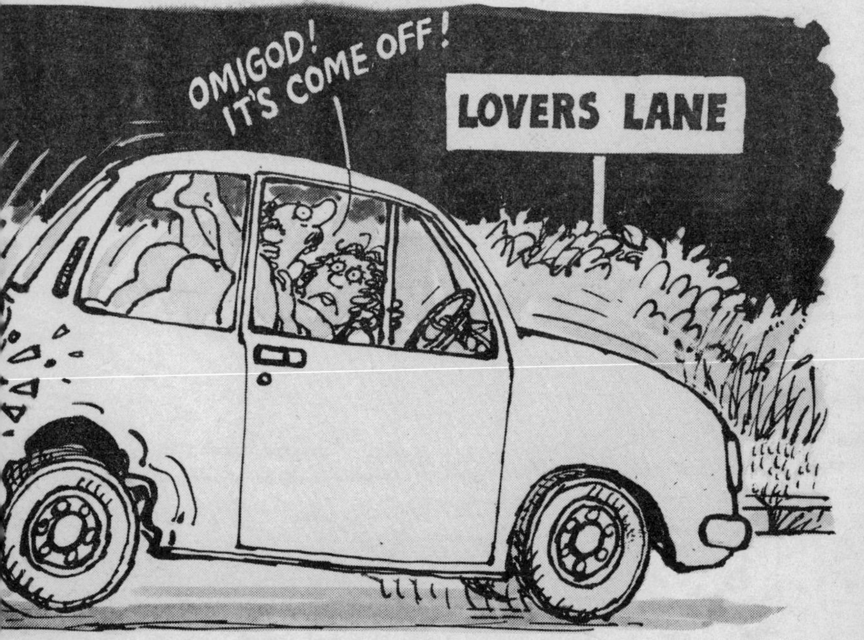

HE WHO LAUGHS LAST HAS TOOTHACHE

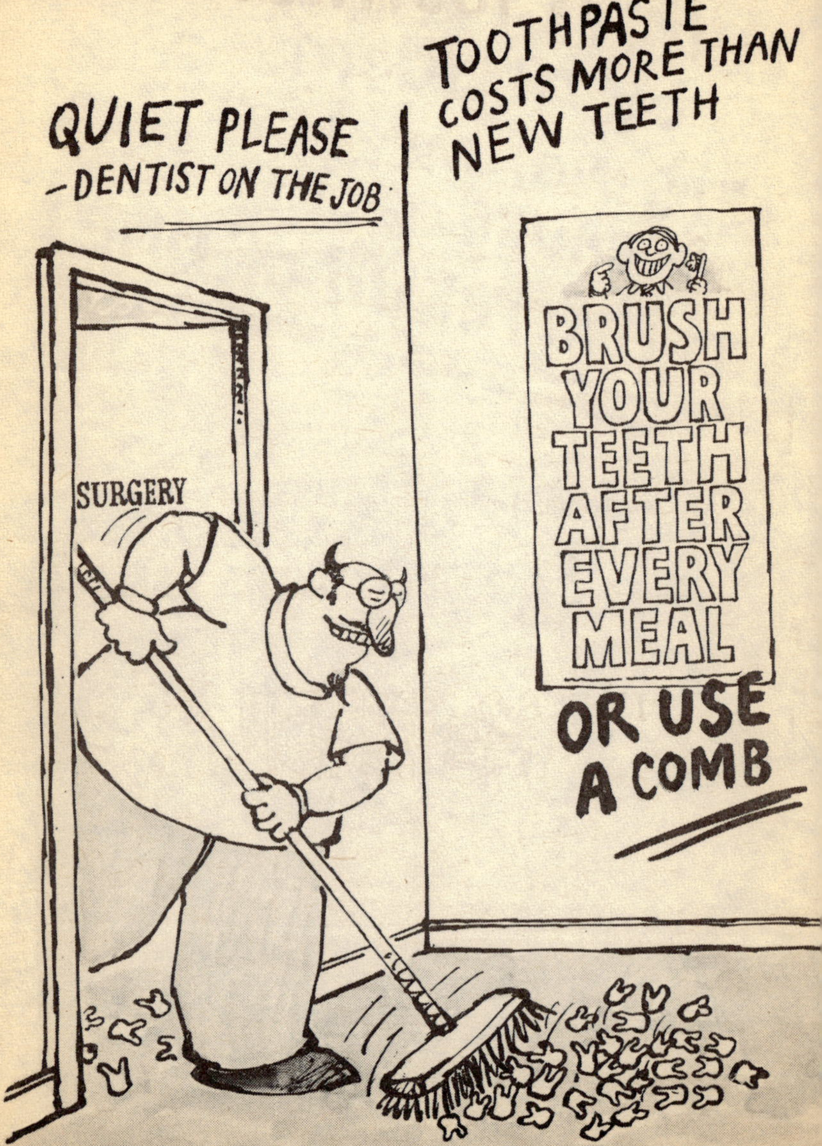

QUIET PLEASE
-DENTIST ON THE JOB

TOOTHPASTE COSTS MORE THAN NEW TEETH

BRUSH YOUR TEETH AFTER EVERY MEAL

OR USE A COMB

SURGERY

Nothing succeeds like a toothless budgie.

STOP YOUR HUSBAND BITING HIS NAILS -HIDE HIS DENTURES.

NO SMOKING IN THE WAITING ROOM ~~OR SCREAMING~~ & SWEATING EITHER

Dentists aren't prejudiced -they hate everyone.

I'M SAVING OLD MAGAZINES. -I'M STUDYING TO BE A DENTIST

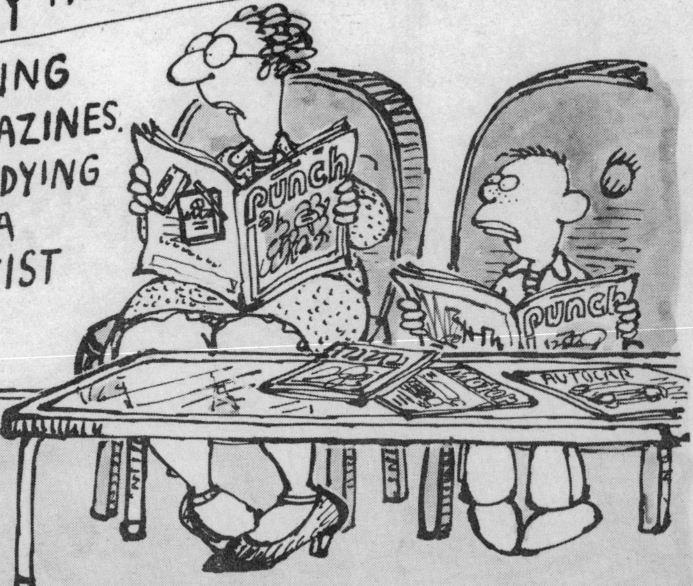

Punch

Punch

AUTOCAR

I'd rather have a baby than have a tooth out.

MAKE UP YOUR MIND, LADY, I'LL HAVE TO ALTER THE POSITION OF THE CHAIR

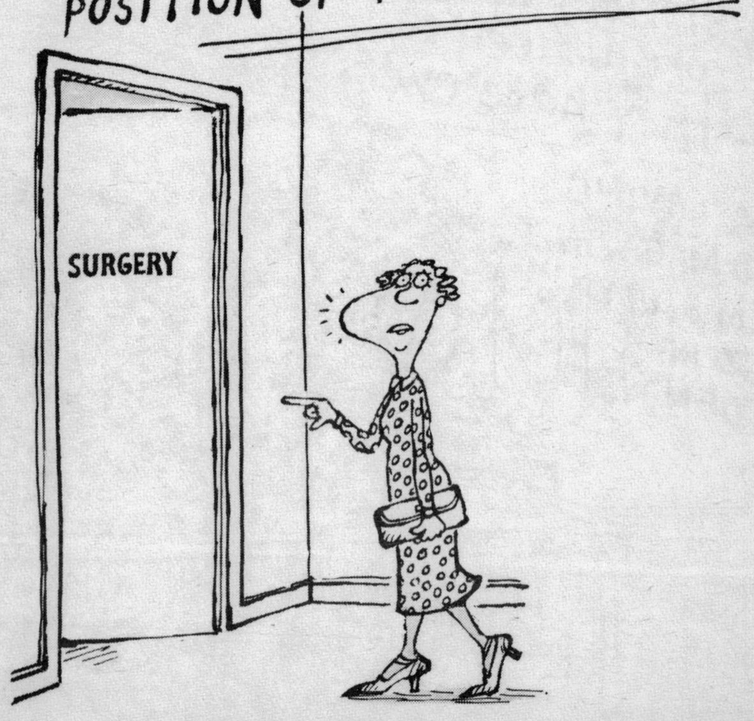

2.30 — Time to go to Chinese dentist.

MY DENTIST IS PAINLESS – HE DOESN'T FEEL A THING.

DENTISTS DO IT ON THE COUCH.

Many a true word is spoken through false teeth

DENTISTS BORE ME TO TEARS

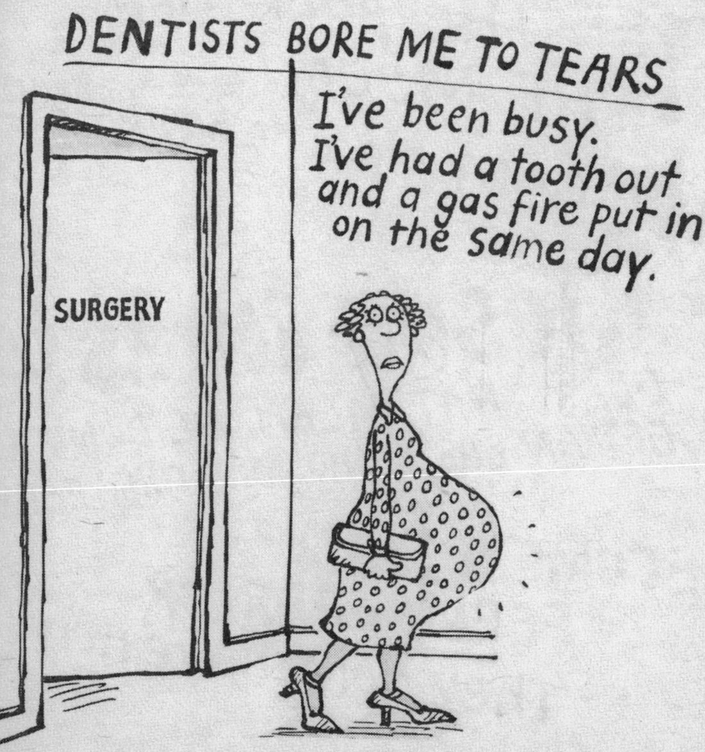

KEEP THE POPE OFF THE MOON

If God exists that's his problem.

KEEP THE POPE OFF THE MOON! It's the only place he hasn't been

Jesus lives! DOES THAT MEAN WE DON'T GET AN EASTER HOLIDAY THIS YEAR?

BECOME A NUN —FEEL SUPERIOR They don't have nun!

GOD IS NOT DEAD
—THIS IS JUST A RUMOUR
PUT AROUND BY PEOPLE WHO
WANT TO BECOME VICARS
AND ONLY WORK ON SUNDAY!

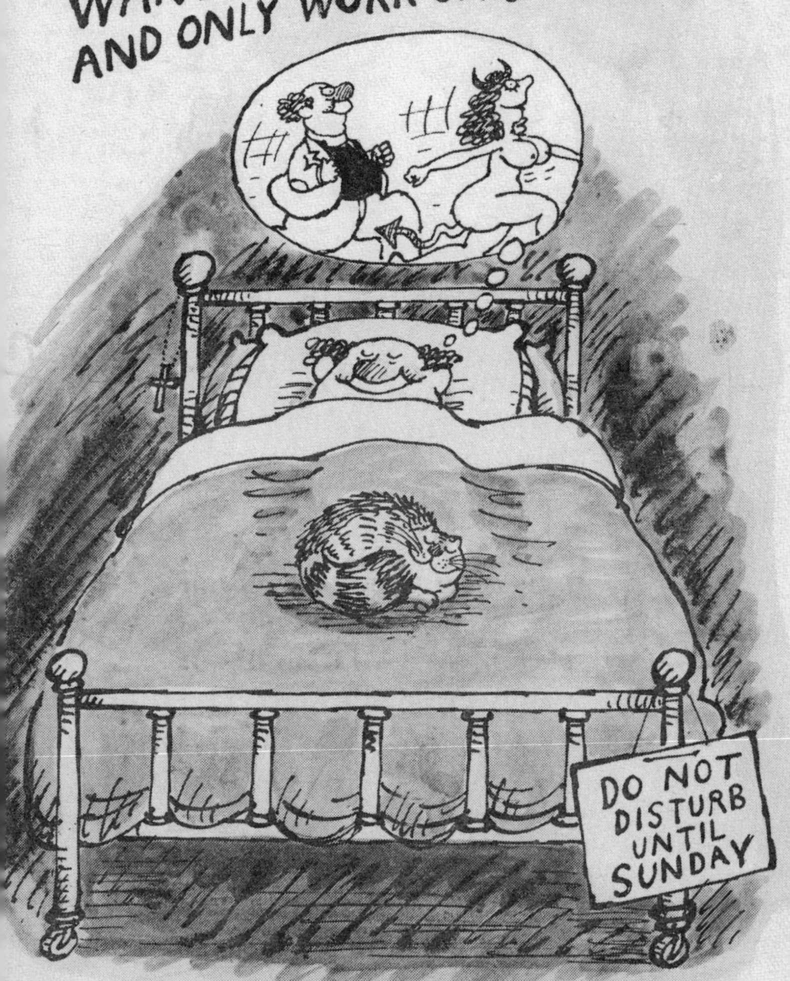

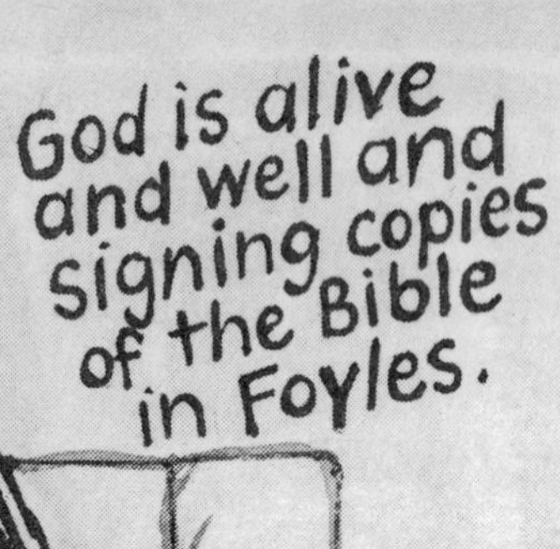

The Lord is my shepherd.

PSALM 23 : 1

BUT WE STILL LOSE THE SHEEPDOG TRIALS

NOTICE

The box marked 'FOR THE SICK' is for monetary contributions only

VICAR

If God hadn't meant us to be racially prejudiced he would have made us all the same colour.

DON'T CRITICISE CLIFF RICHARD – YOU MIGHT BE A VIRGIN YOURSELF ONE DAY.

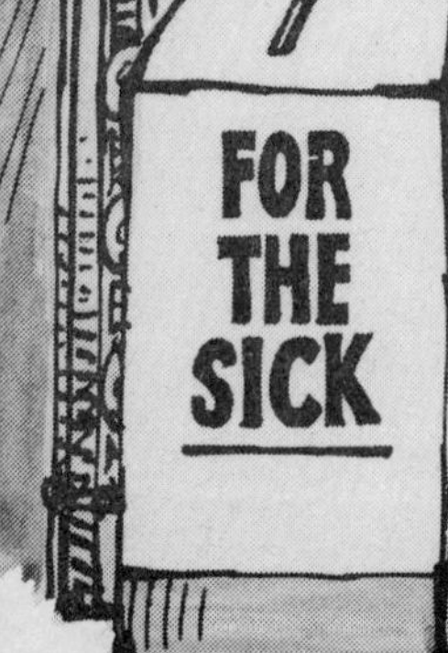

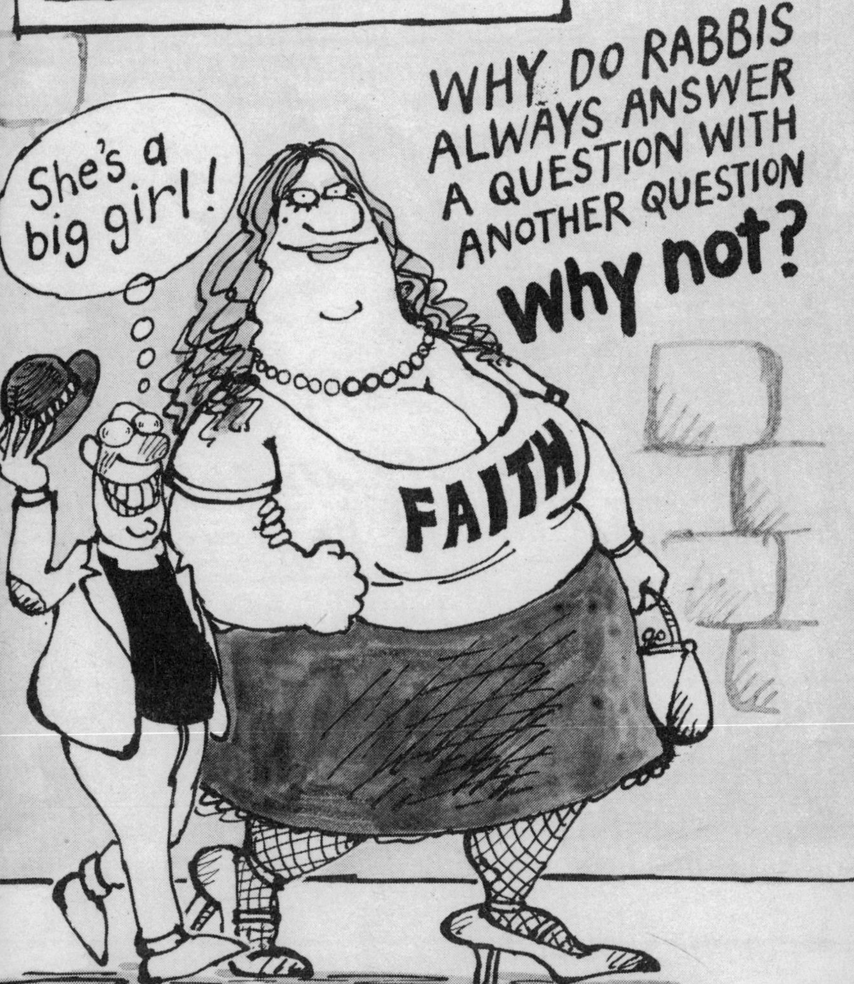
FAITH CAN MOVE MOUNTAINS.
She's a big girl!
FAITH
WHY DO RABBIS ALWAYS ANSWER A QUESTION WITH ANOTHER QUESTION
Why not?

REALITY IS AN ILLUSION CAUSED BY LACK OF ALCOHOL

TRY CIDER
WITH ROSÉ.

I'M RICH! I'M RICH!
I'VE JUST DISCOVERED
W.C. FIELDS' EMPTIES!

W.C. Fields was only
drunk once in his life—
He was stoned out of
his mind for the rest.

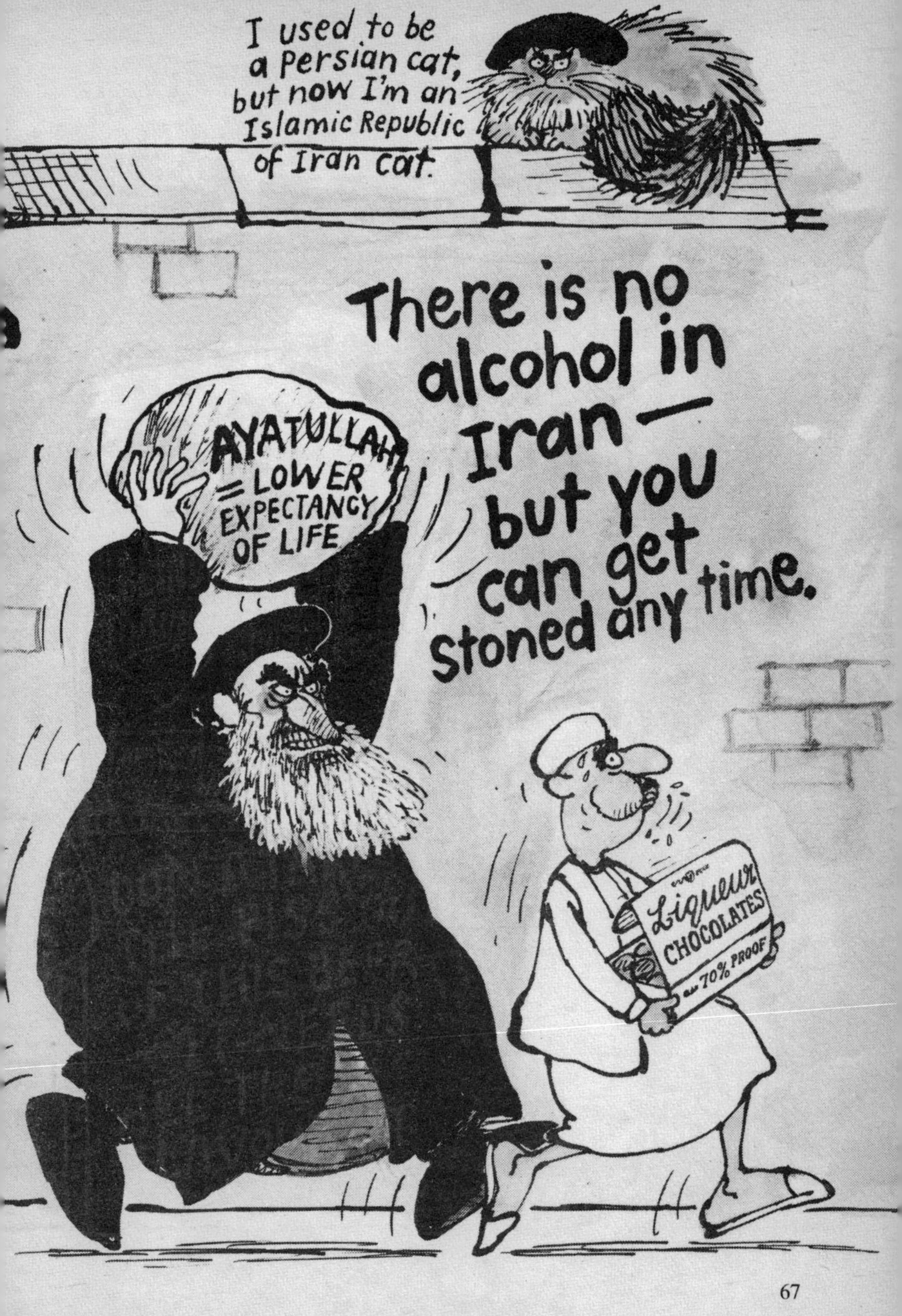

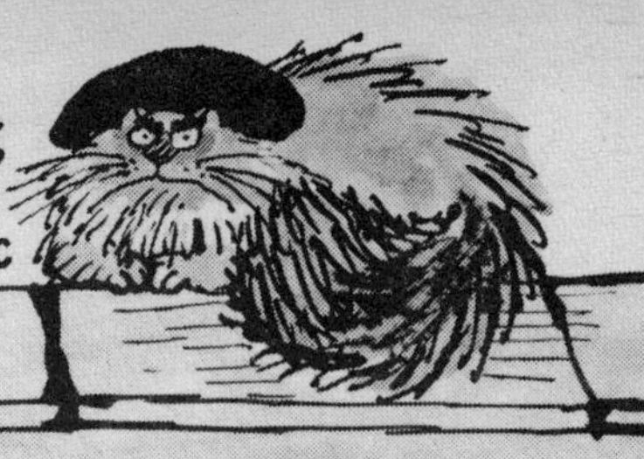

There is no alcohol in Iran — but you can get stoned any time.

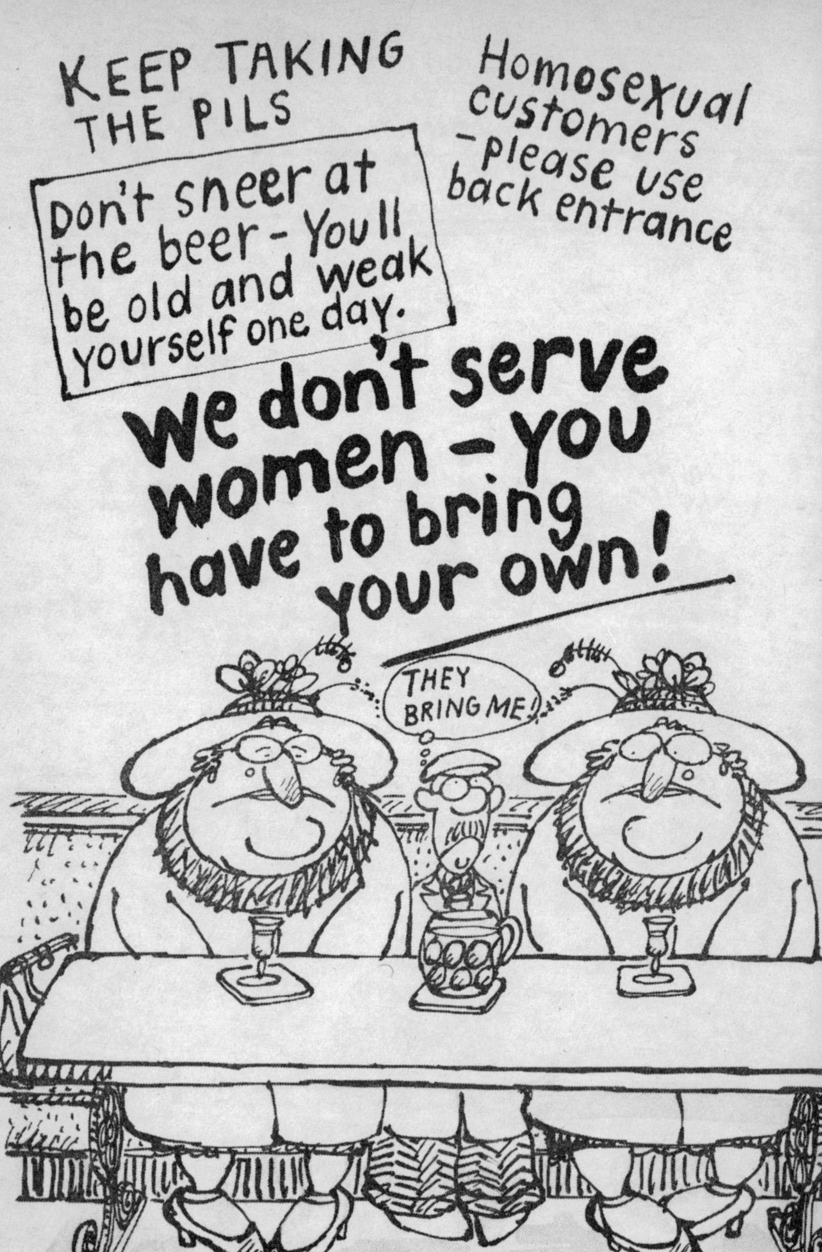
KEEP TAKING THE PILS
Homosexual customers -please use back entrance
Don't sneer at the beer - You'll be old and weak yourself one day.
We don't serve women - you have to bring your own!
THEY BRING ME!

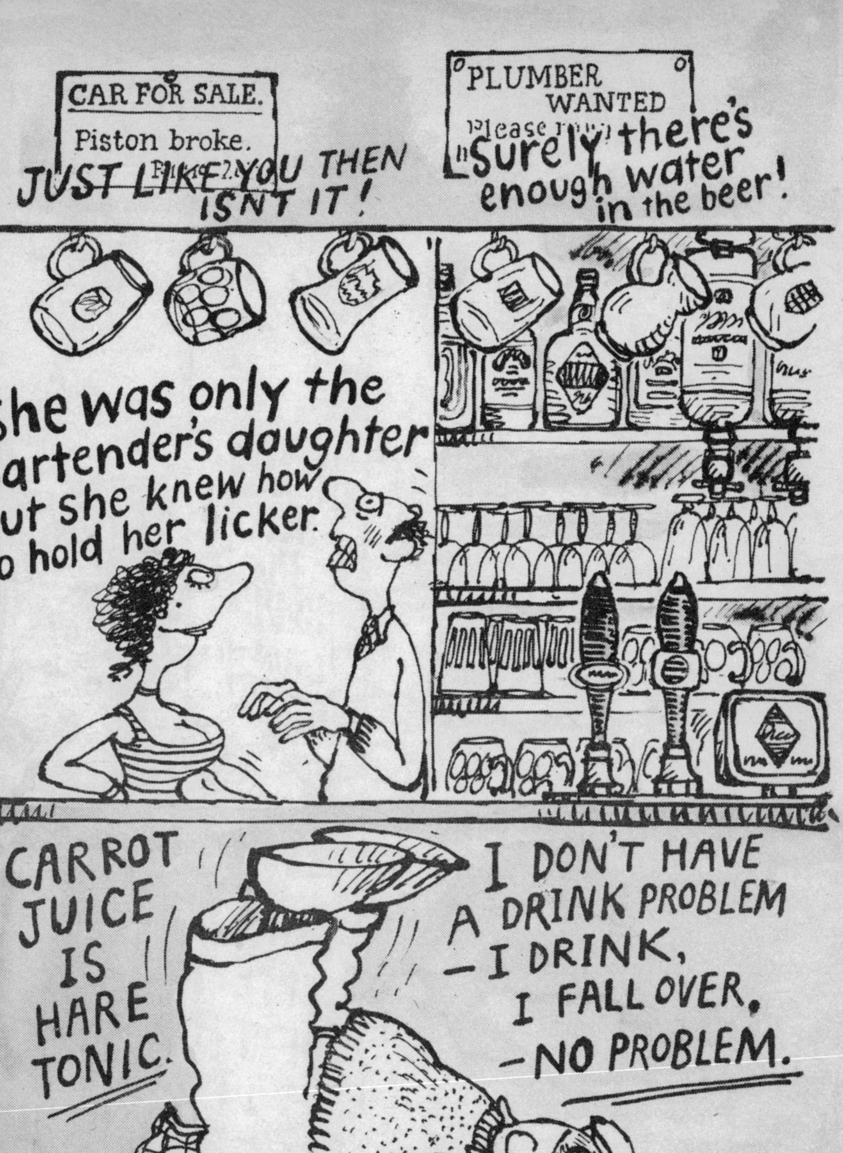
CAR FOR SALE.
Piston broke.
JUST LIKE YOU THEN ISNT IT!
PLUMBER WANTED
"Surely there's enough water in the beer!
She was only the bartender's daughter but she knew how to hold her licker.
CARROT JUICE IS HARE TONIC.
I DON'T HAVE A DRINK PROBLEM
– I DRINK, I FALL OVER.
– NO PROBLEM.

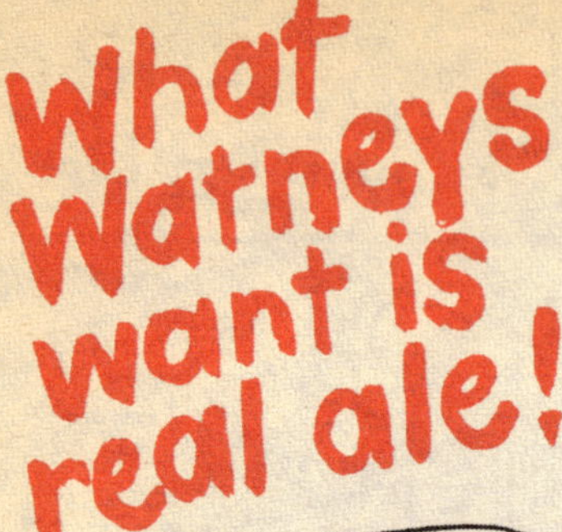
What Watneys want is real ale!

I've a drink problem – I can't afford it!

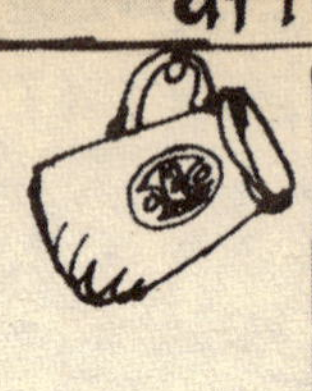

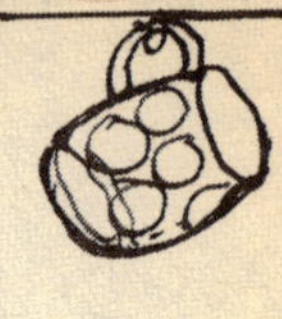

Blessed are the weak in gravity for they shall be reviled by CAMRA.

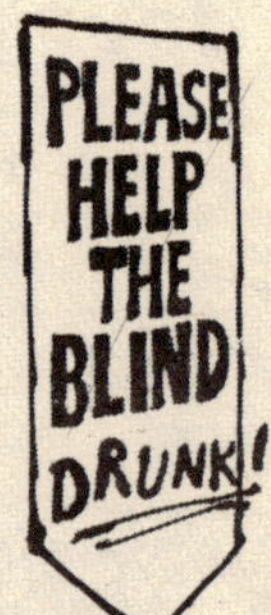
PLEASE HELP THE BLIND
DRUNK!

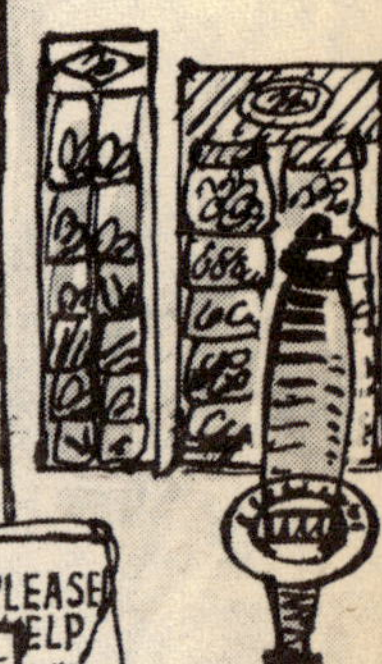

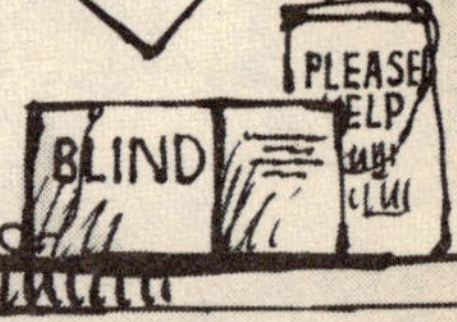
BLIND
PLEASE

DON'T TAKE THE PISS OUT OF THIS BEER – IT NEEDS ALL THE FLAVOUR IT CAN GET!

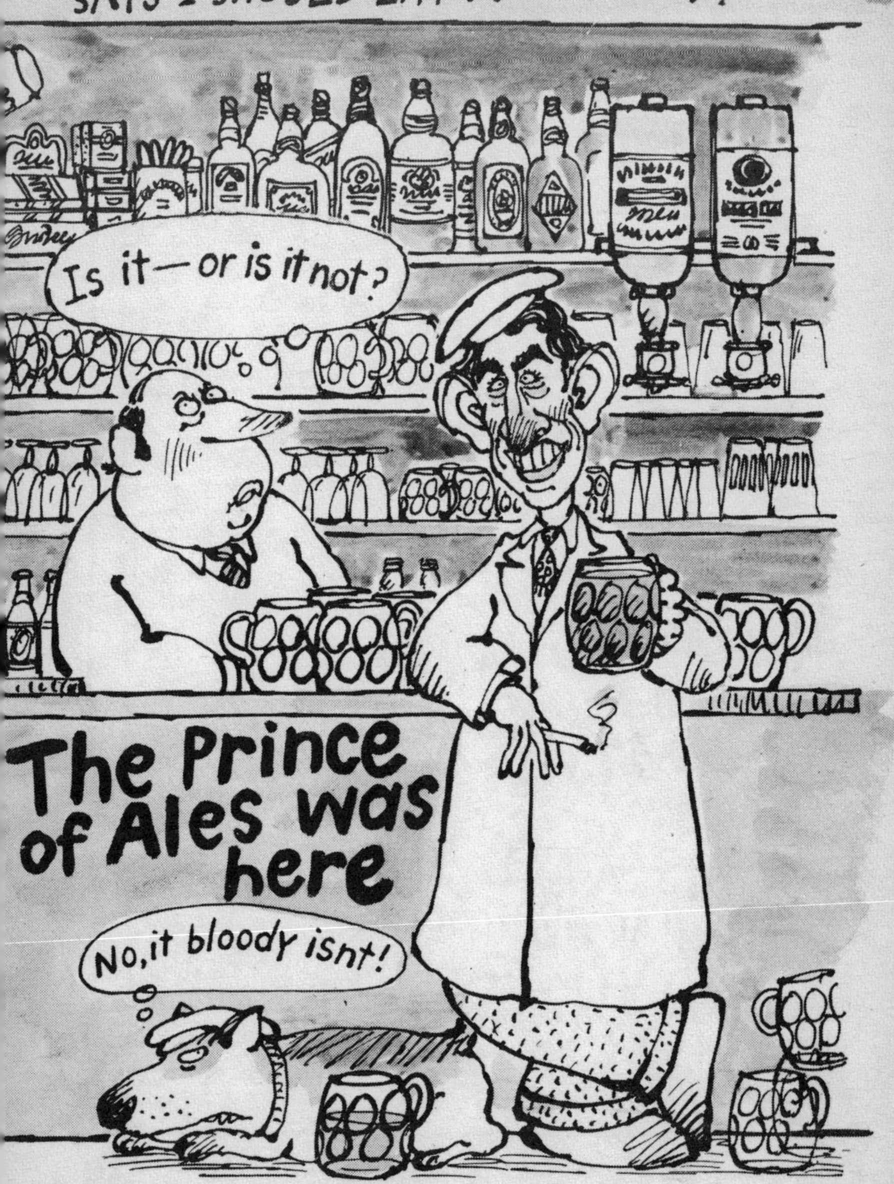
PUT TWO CHERRIES IN MY BEER – THE DOCTOR SAYS I SHOULD EAT MORE FRUIT.!
Is it — or is it not?
The Prince of Ales was here
No, it bloody isnt!

TWO'S COMPANY, THREE'S A DEFORMITY

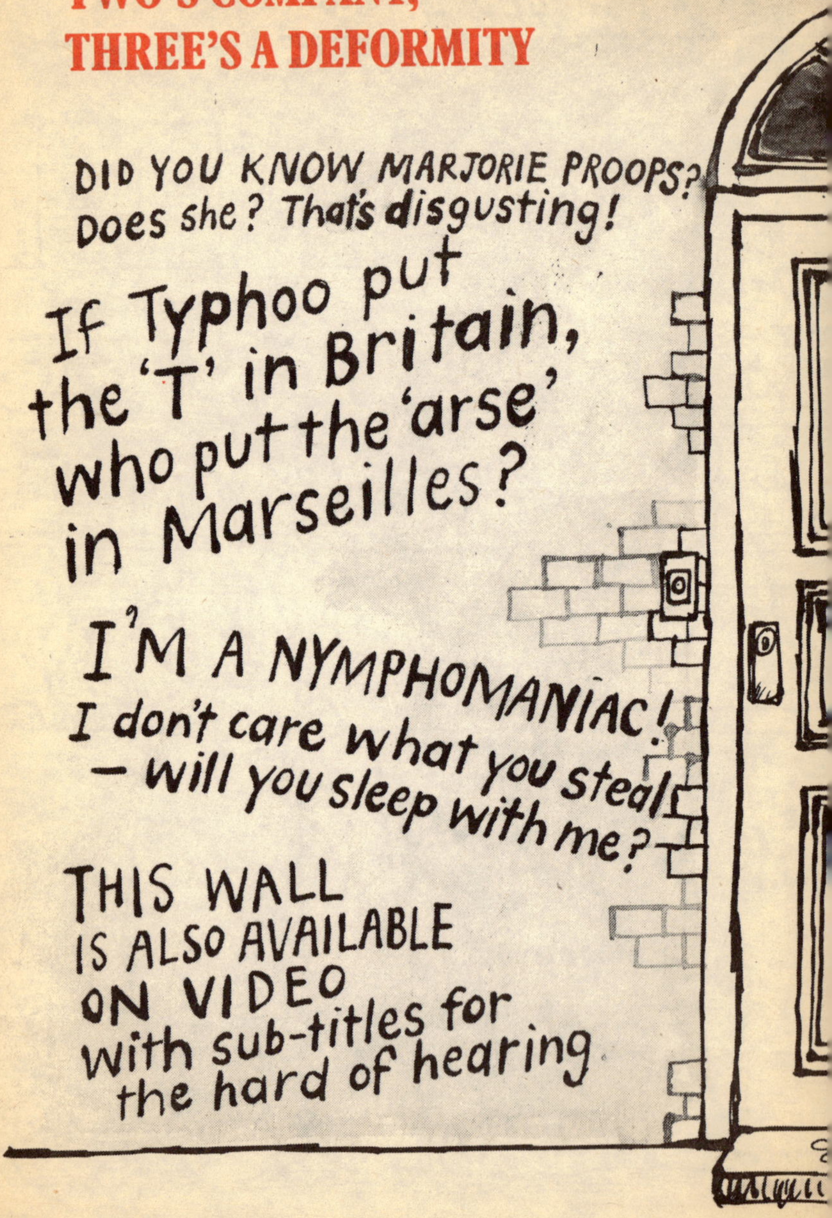

DID YOU KNOW MARJORIE PROOPS?
Does she? That's disgusting!

If Typhoo put
the 'T' in Britain,
who put the 'arse'
in Marseilles?

I'M A NYMPHOMANIAC!
I don't care what you steal
– will you sleep with me?

THIS WALL
IS ALSO AVAILABLE
ON VIDEO
with sub-titles for
the hard of hearing

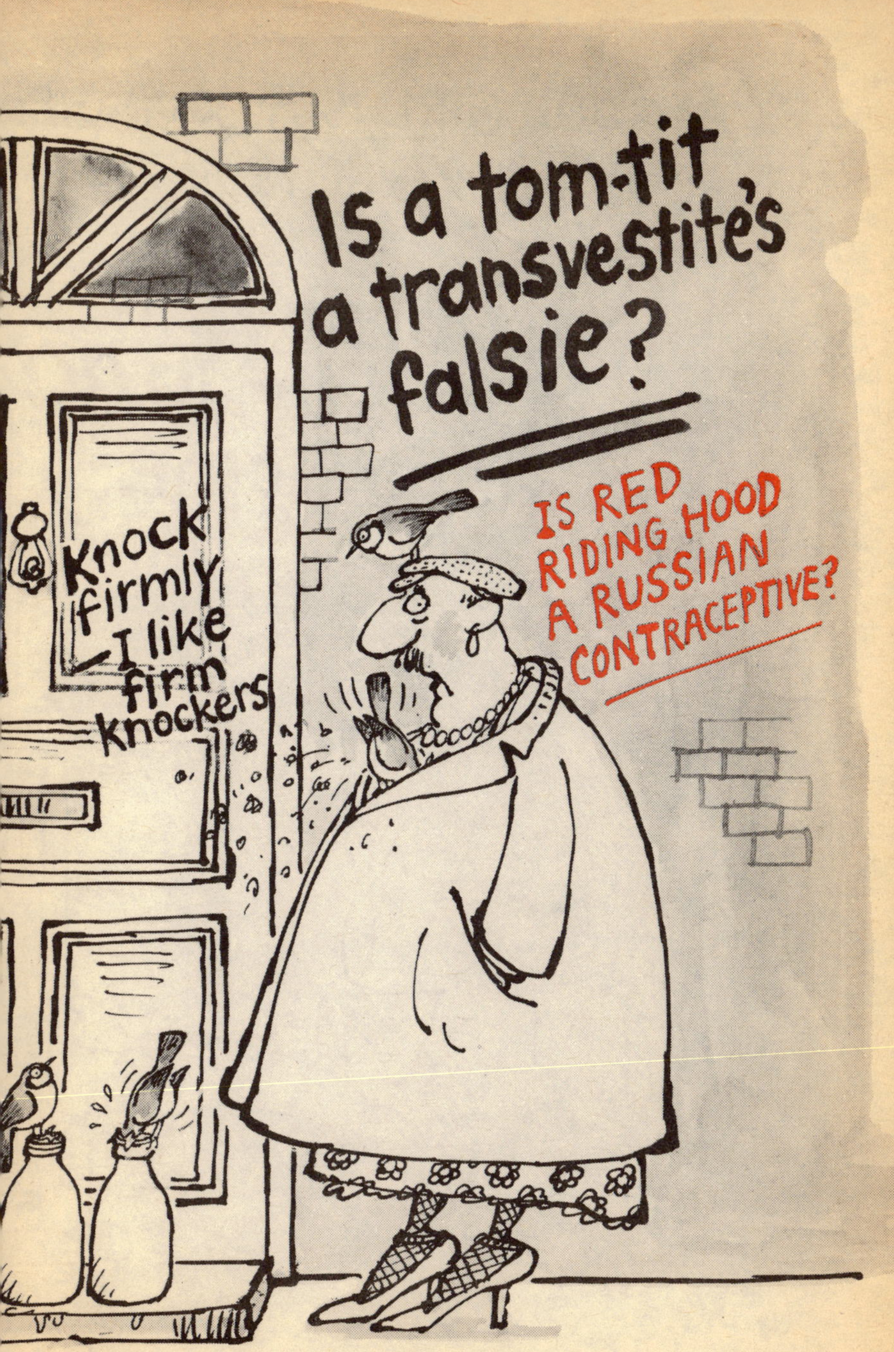
Is a tom-tit a transvestite's falsie?
IS RED RIDING HOOD A RUSSIAN CONTRACEPTIVE?
Knock firmly – I like firm knockers

A GOOD GIRL IS A GOOD GIRL
-BUT A BAD GIRL IS BETTER.

My mum says if I'm not in bed by 10.30, I'm to go home.

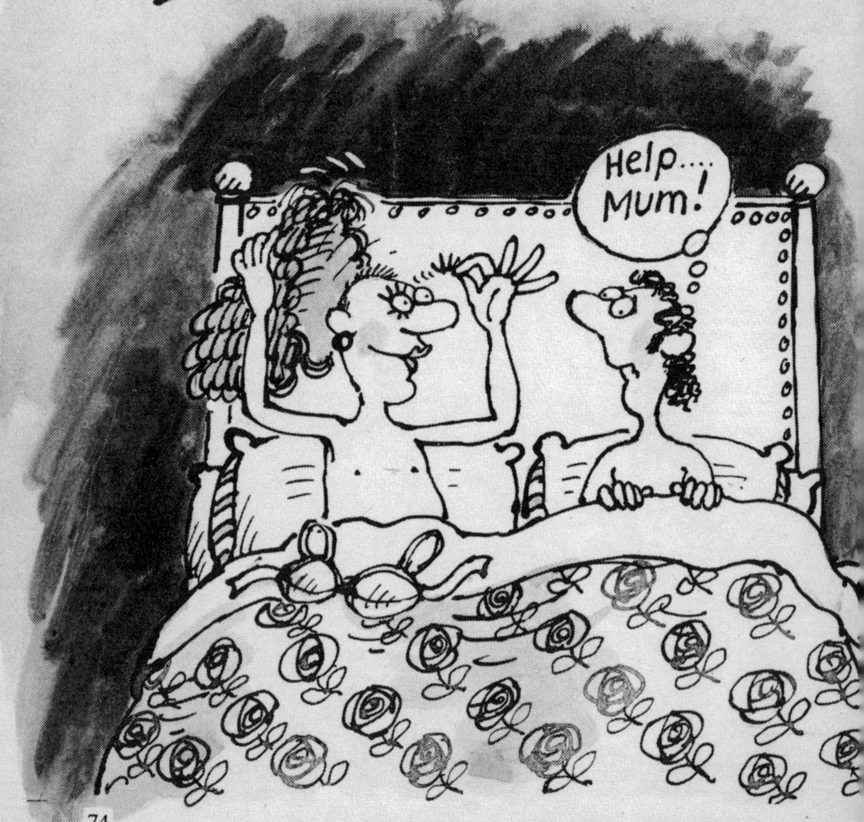

Never kiss at the garden gate.
Love is blind but the neighbours aint.

I'VE DONE IT 144 TIMES!
THAT'S GROSS INDECENCY!

I believe in moderation in small doses.

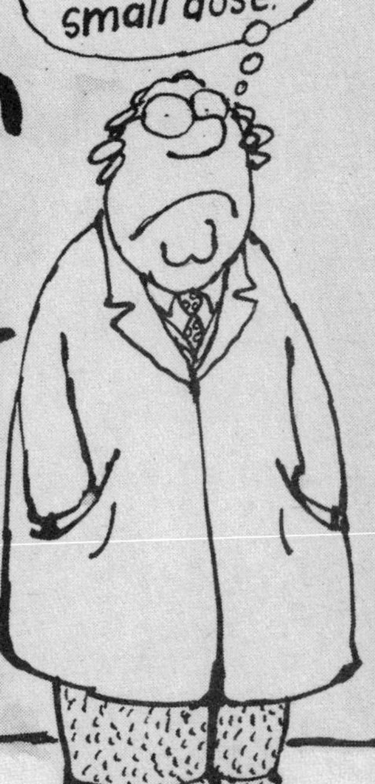

EVE WAS FRAMED!

A MAN CAN NEVER TELL ABOU
A GIRL UNTIL HE IS ALONE
WITH HER BEHIND THE BIK
SHEDS – AFTER THAT HE SHOULDN'

If a guy prefers blondes,
it doesn't mean he's
a gentleman.

EXPERIMENT TO
FIND OUT WHETHER
PICKLED ONIONS ARE
ILLEGITIMATE.
UNSCREW THE LID
TURN THE JAR
UPSIDE DOWN AND
ALL THE LITTLE
BASTARDS DROP OUT!

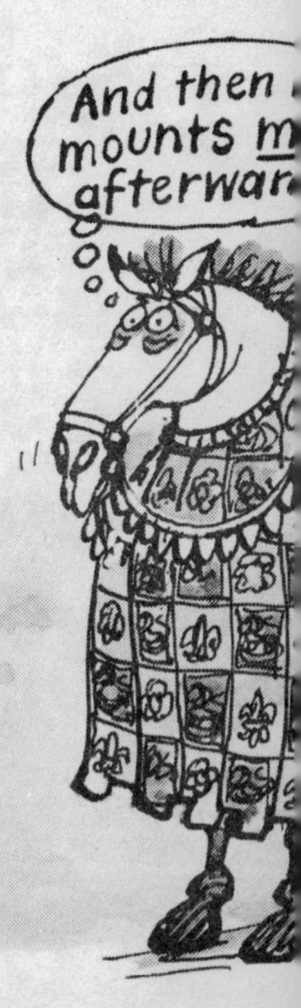

The Grand Old Duke of York,
He had 10,000 men
-HIS CASE COMES UP NEXT WEEK.

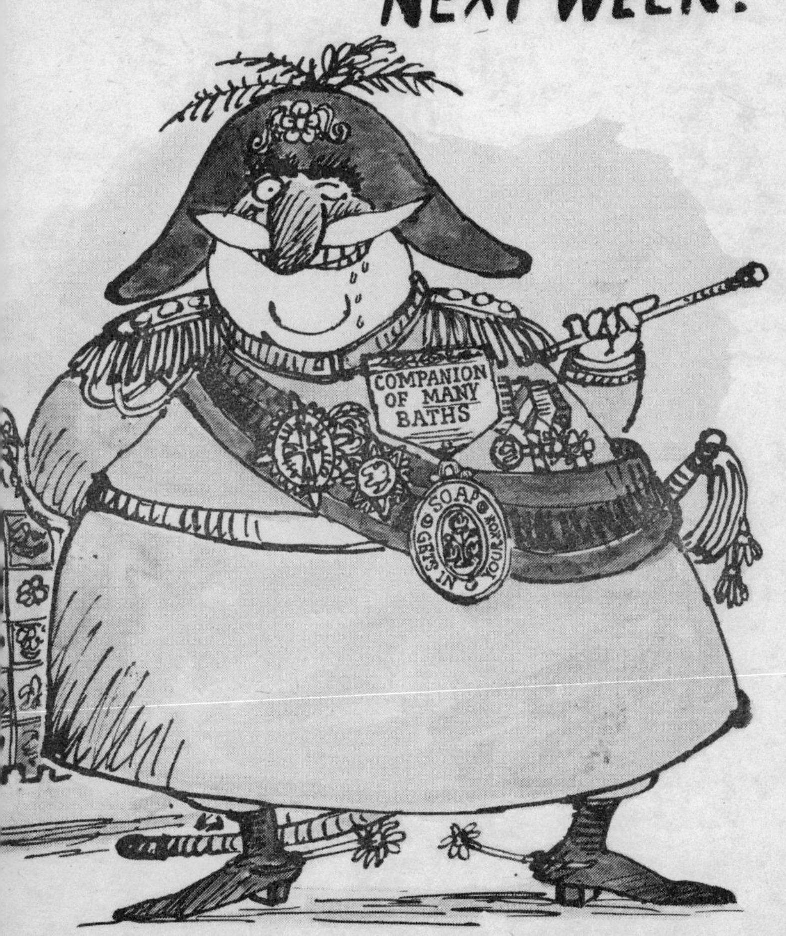

GIVE BLOOD – PLAY RUGBY!

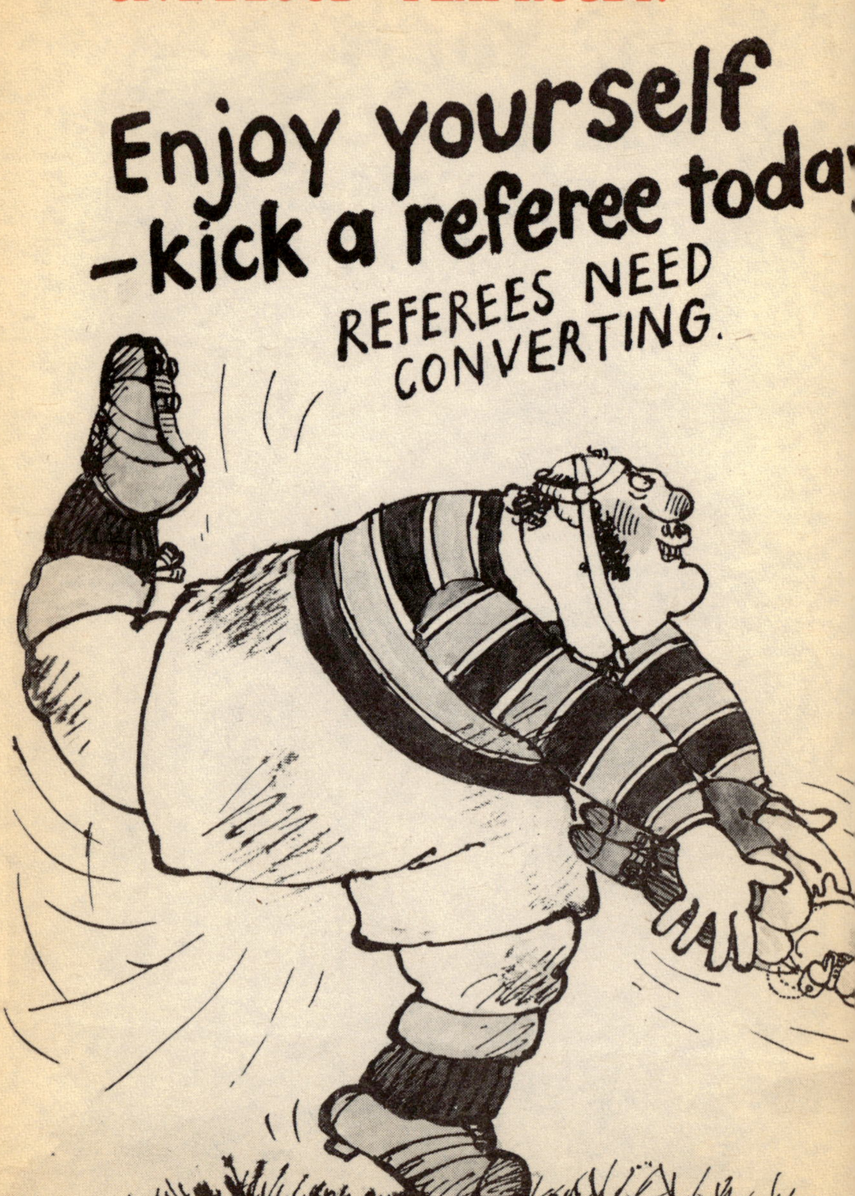

OLD RUGBY PLAYERS NEVER DIE. THEY SIMPLY HAVE THEIR BALLS TAKEN AWAY.

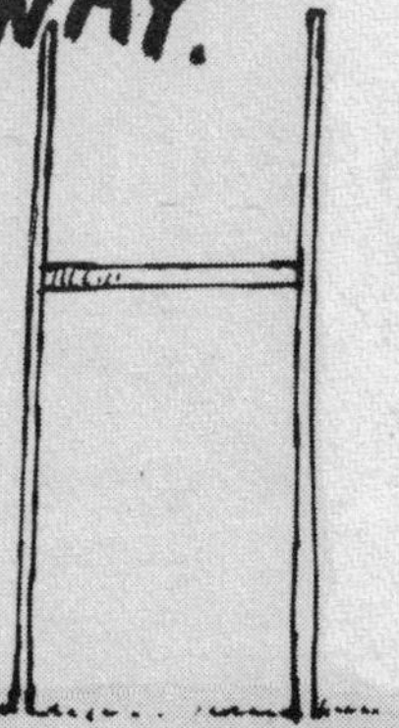

Rugby is a colourful game— you get black and blue all over

RUGBY IS LIKE INCEST - A GAME FOR ALL THE FAMILY.

You need leather balls to play rugby.

Women are like British Rail coffe
— Weak with two lumps!
MEN ARE LIKE CLUB HOUSE COFFE
— STRONG WITH ONE LUMP!

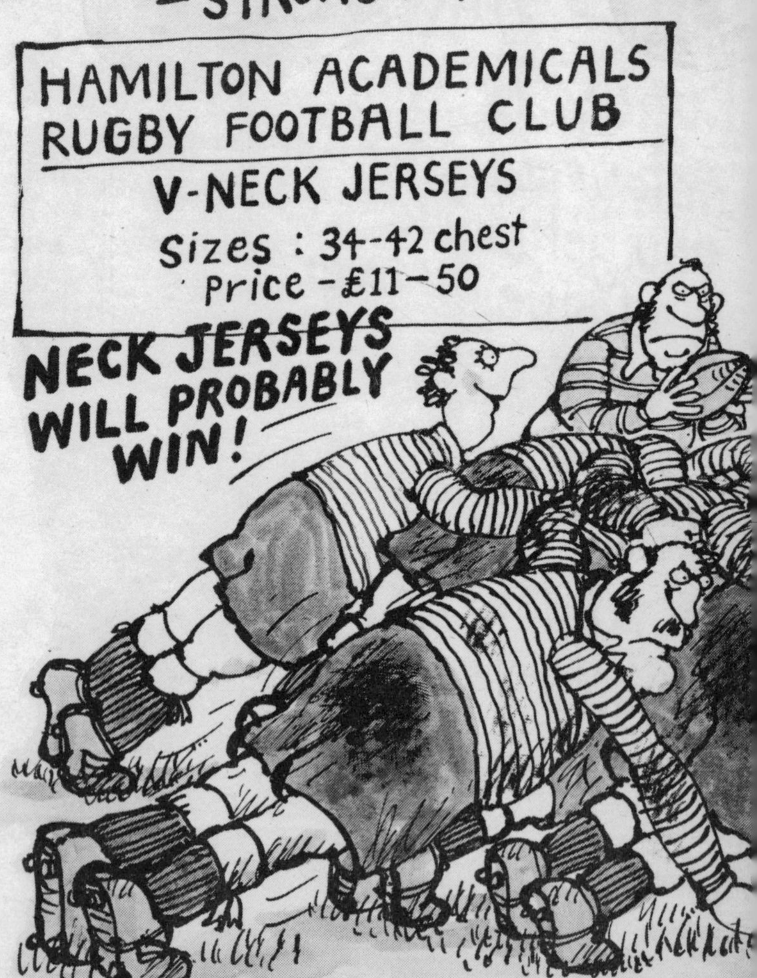

WHAT'S WHITE AND SLITHERS ACROSS THE FLOOR?
— COME DANCING!

Man cannot live on bread alone
— He needs a bit of crumpet.

Play rugby
-legalise cannibalism!

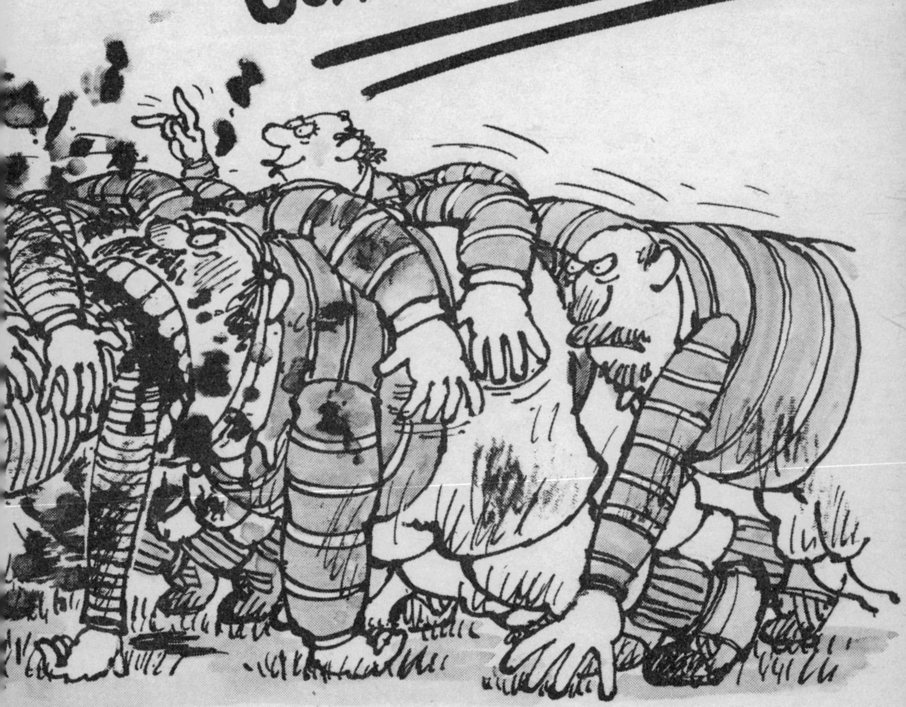

FLIES SPREAD DISEASE
— SO KEEP YOURS SHUT!

The best part of
a game of rugby is
the shower afterwar

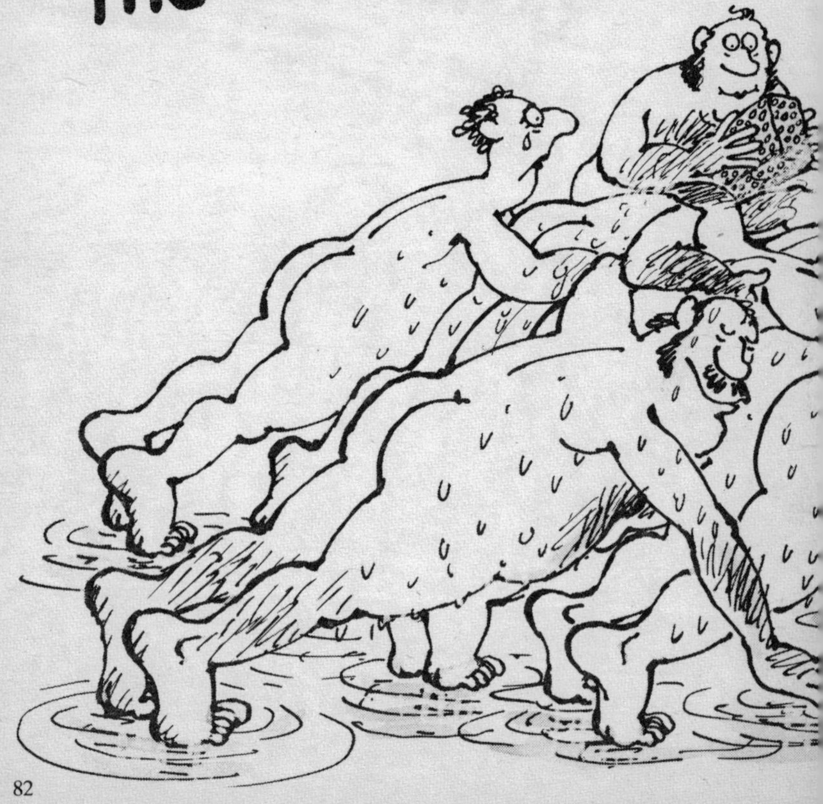

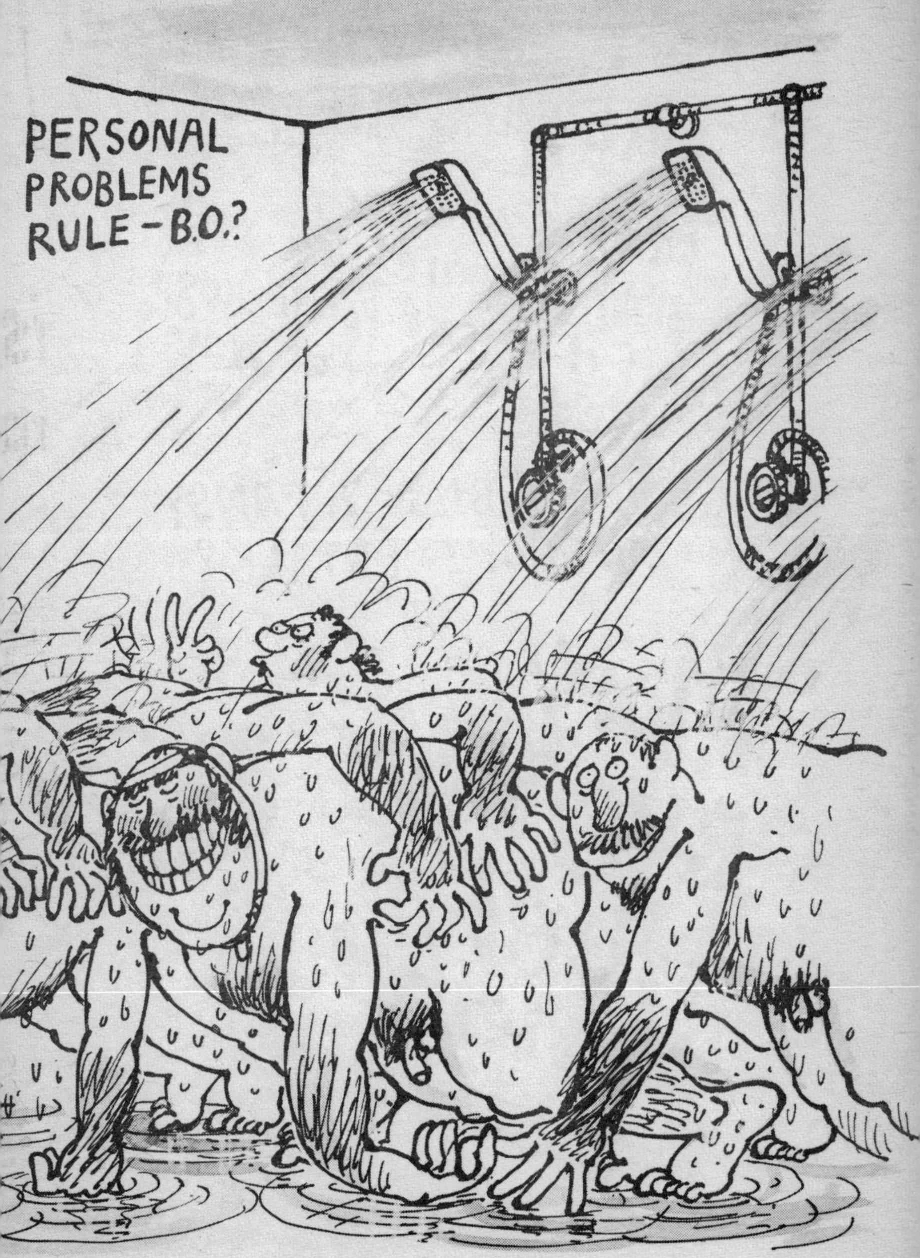
PERSONAL
PROBLEMS
RULE - B.O.?

ANTI-SOCIAL DISEASES ARE A SORE POINT!

Roses are red,
Pansies are gay.
If it wasn't for ladies,
We'd all be that way.

IS A LESBIAN A PANSY WITHOUT A STALK?

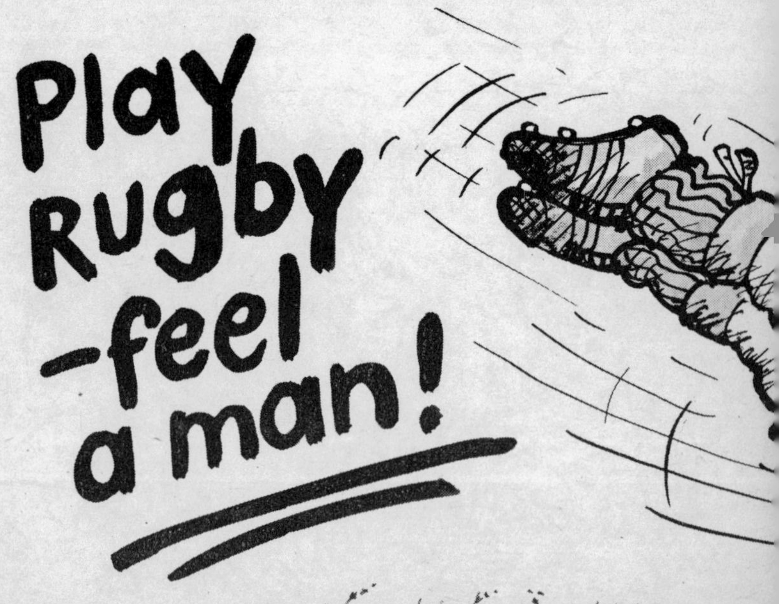

Never fall in love with a tennis player. To them love means nothing.

RUGBY PLAYERS GET A BIG KICK OUT OF IT.

Squash players do it against a wall!

Scrabble players can lay seven at one go!

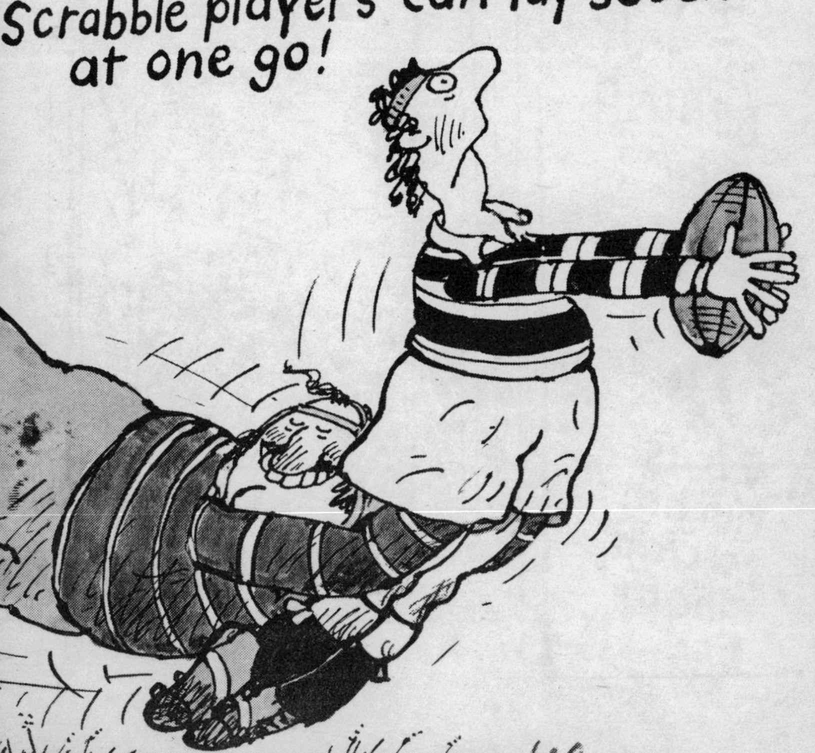

TOILETS ARE WORTH EVERY PENNY SPENT ON THEM

BLACK IS BEAUTIFUL

Then you'll just love these toilets.

WOMEN'S LIBBERS SHOULD BE PUT BEHIND BRAS.

VENI VICI VD

VD is nothing to clap about

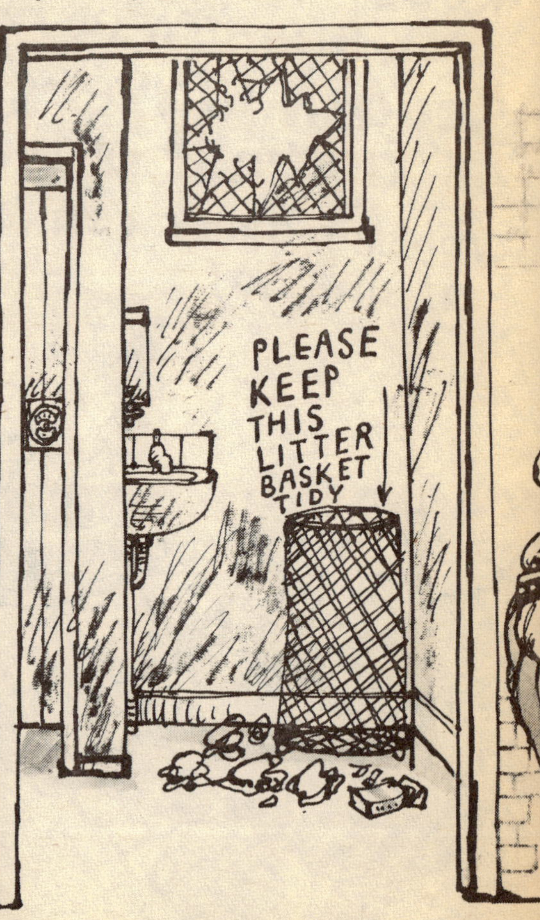

HOME IS HEAVEN
ORGIES ARE VILE.
BUT I LIKE AN ORGY
ONCE IN A WHILE.

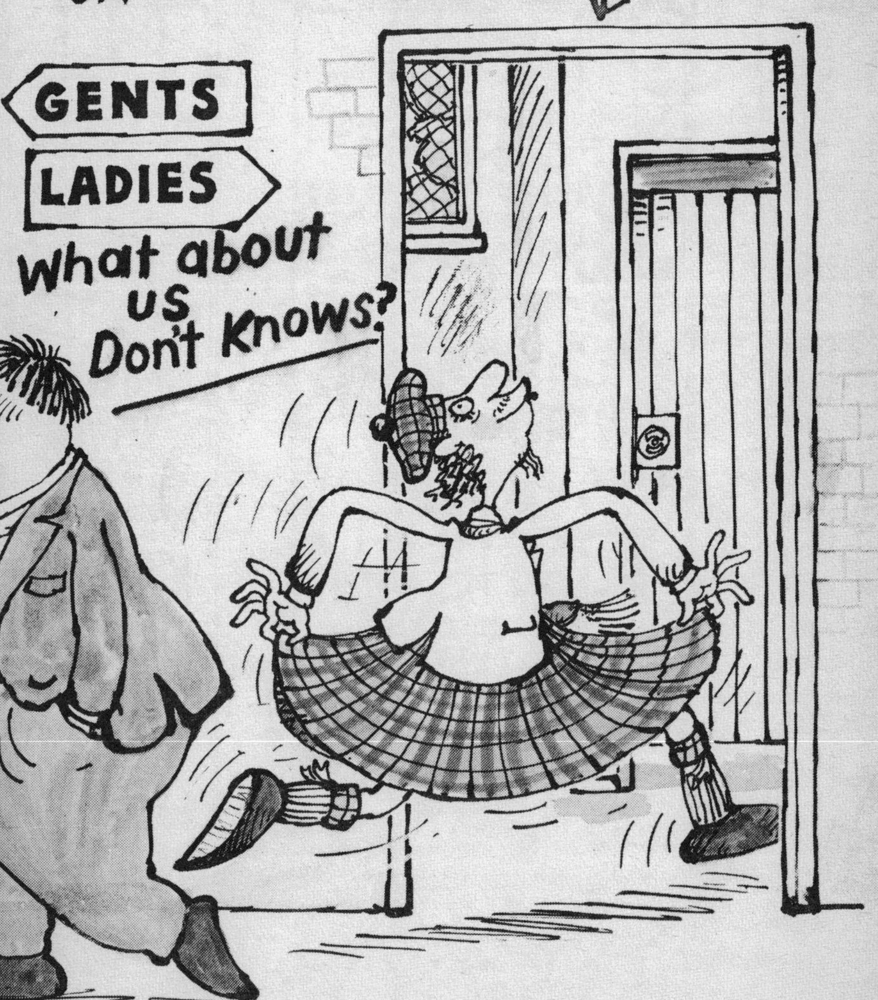

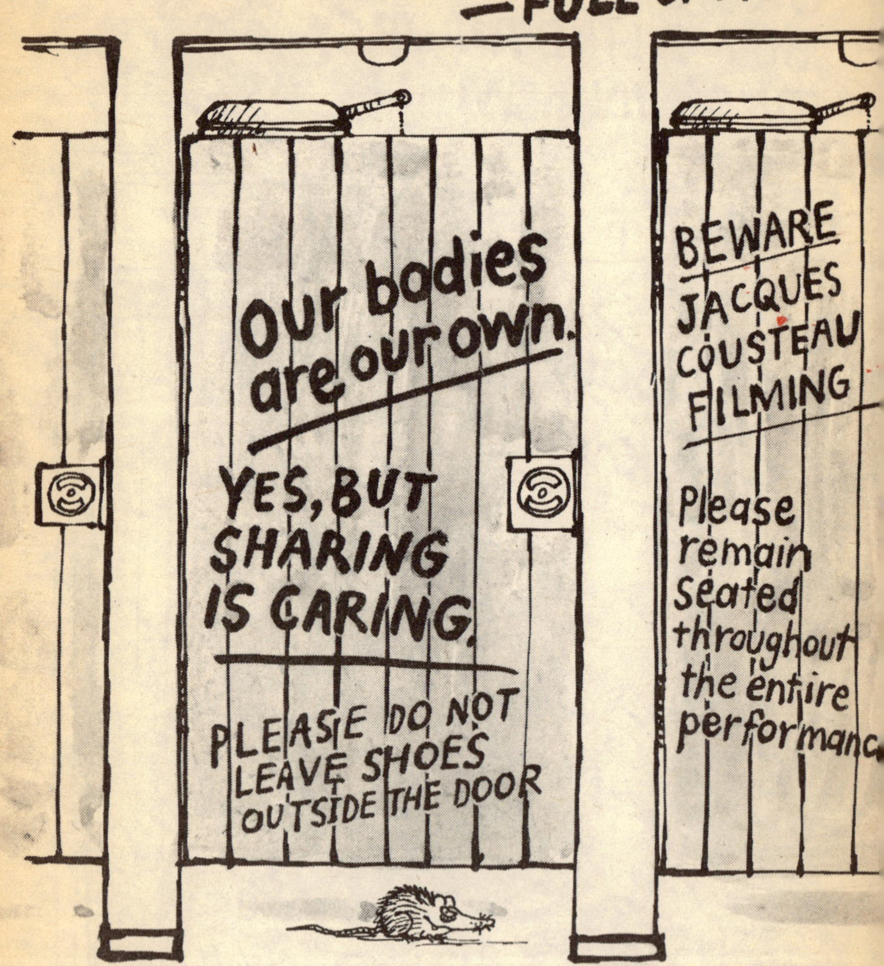
LIFE IS LIKE A BED OF ROSES
—FULL OF PRICKS
Our bodies are our own.
YES, BUT SHARING IS CARING.
PLEASE DO NOT LEAVE SHOES OUTSIDE THE DOOR
BEWARE
JACQUES COUSTEAU FILMING
Please remain seated throughout the entire performanc

Toilet paper is supplied by the Master of the Rolls.

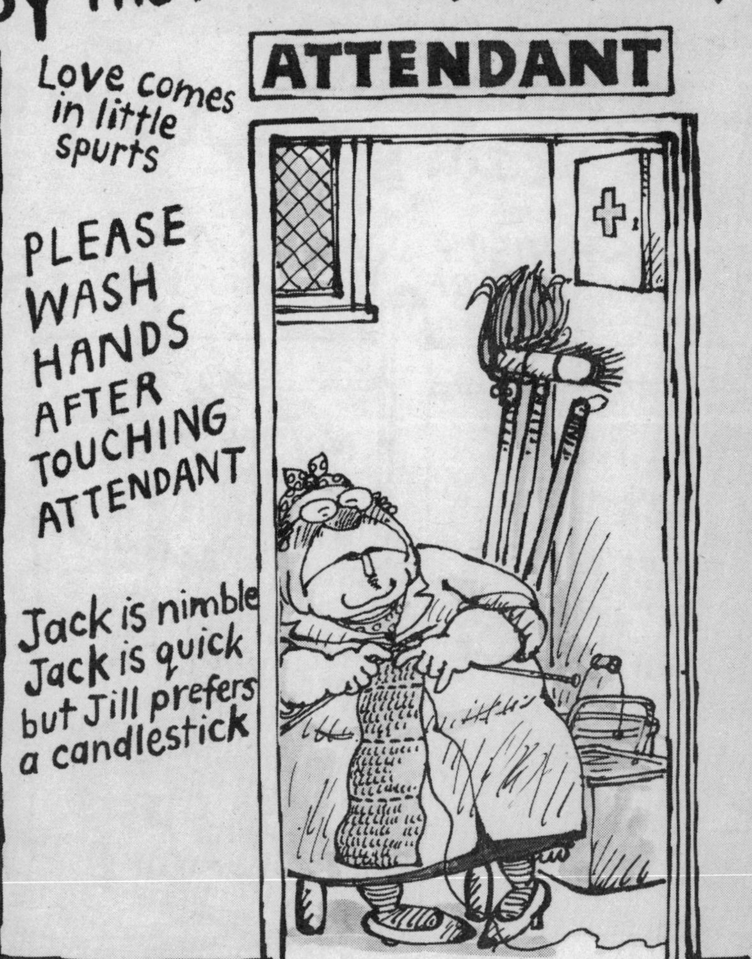

BE BI-SEXUAL
AND DOUBLE YOUR CHANCES

I'm bi-sexual.
If I can't get it, I buy it!

MASOCHISTS DEMAND A
FAIR CRACK OF THE WHIP

Annual
Sex Orgy
here on
Friday–
First served,
First come.

My brother's
is only half
an inch—
off the ground!

WHAT'S THE
DIFFERENCE
BETWEEN
TRUE LOVE AND
HERPES?
Herpes lasts
forever!

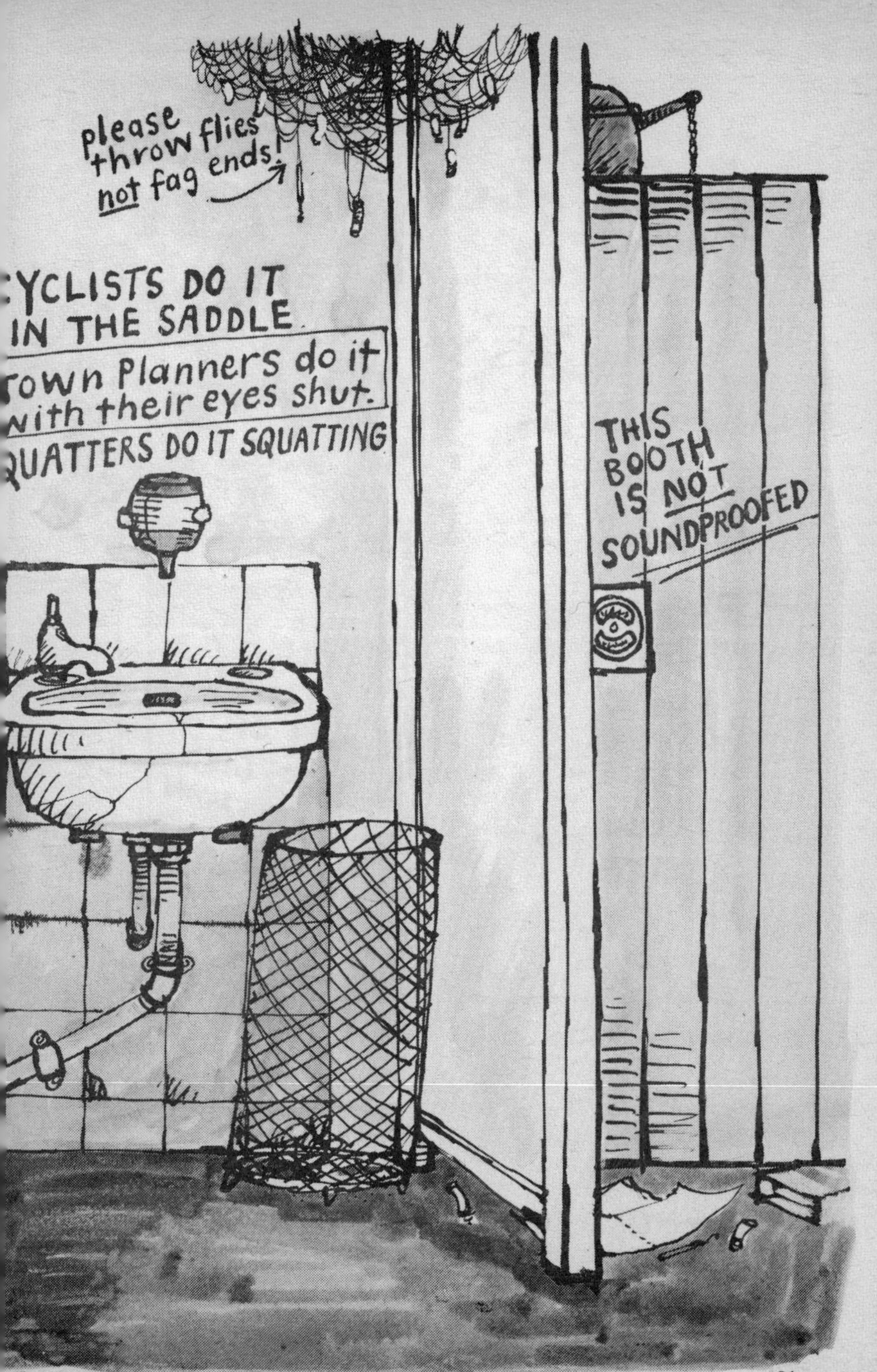
please throw flies not fag ends!
CYCLISTS DO IT IN THE SADDLE
Town Planners do it with their eyes shut.
QUATTERS DO IT SQUATTING
THIS BOOTH IS NOT SOUNDPROOFED

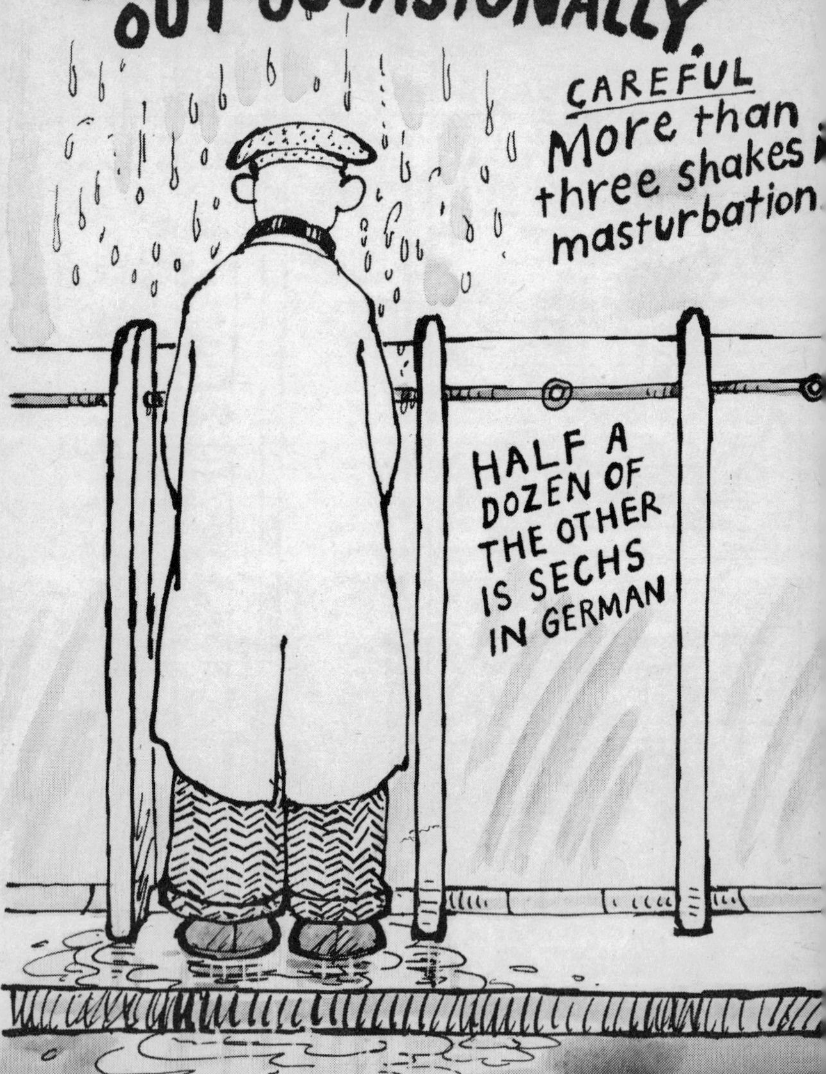
I LIKE TO SPLASH OUT OCCASIONALLY.
CAREFUL
More than
three shakes
masturbation
HALF A
DOZEN OF
THE OTHER
IS SECHS
IN GERMAN

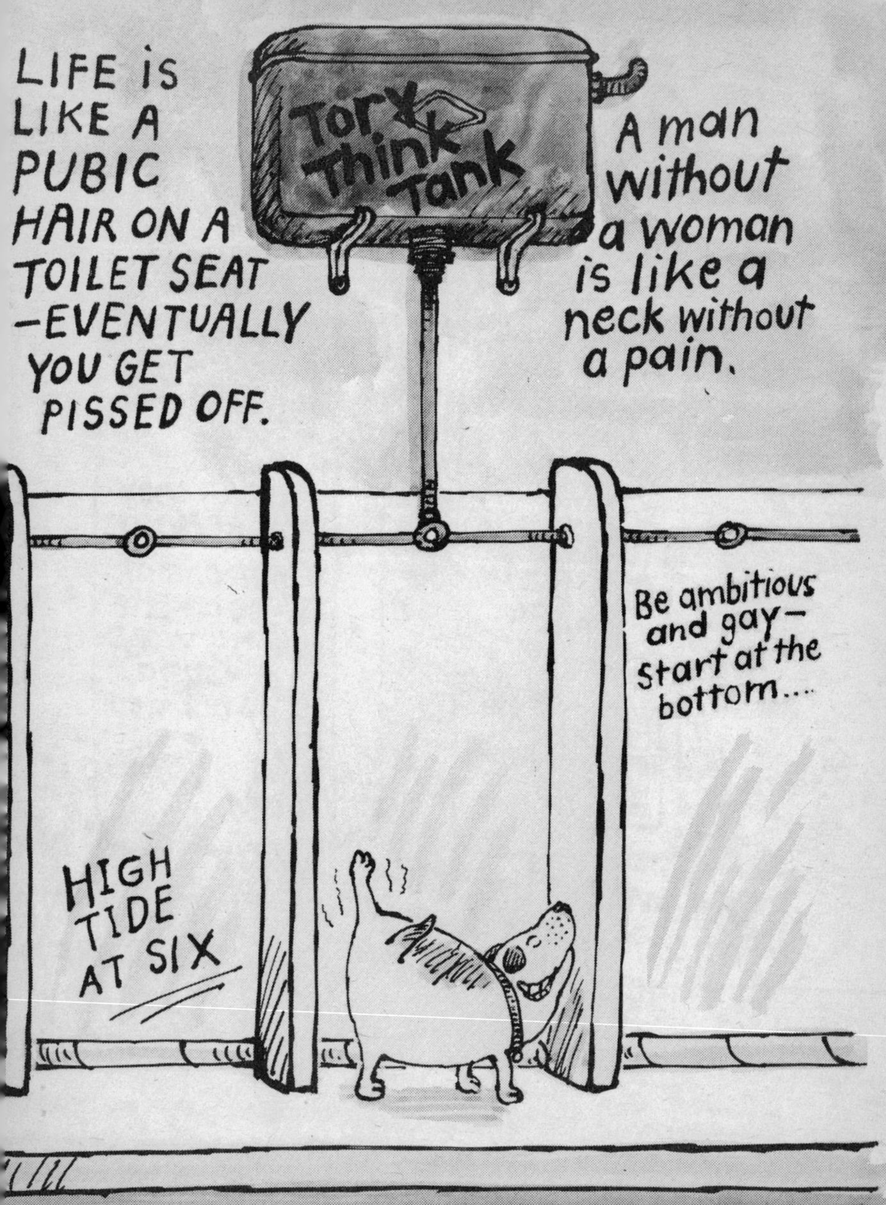
LIFE is LIKE A PUBIC HAIR ON A TOILET SEAT -EVENTUALLY YOU GET PISSED OFF.
Tory Think Tank
A man without a woman is like a neck without a pain.
Be ambitious and gay- start at the bottom....
HIGH TIDE AT SIX

Is Johnny Cash change from a Durex machine?

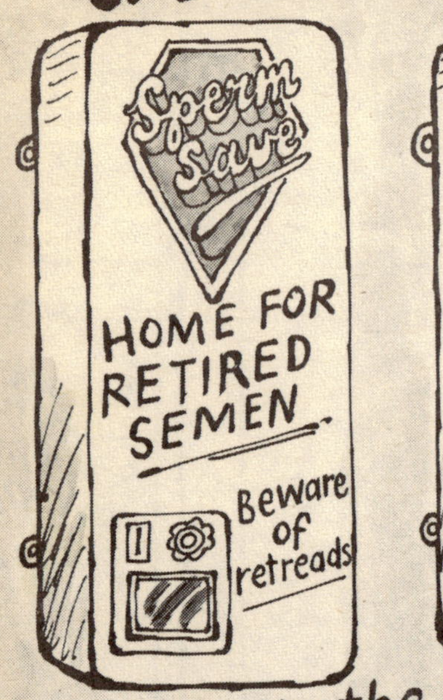

She was only the roadmaker's daughter but she liked her asphalt.

PREVENT CHILDREN —MARRY A LESBIAN

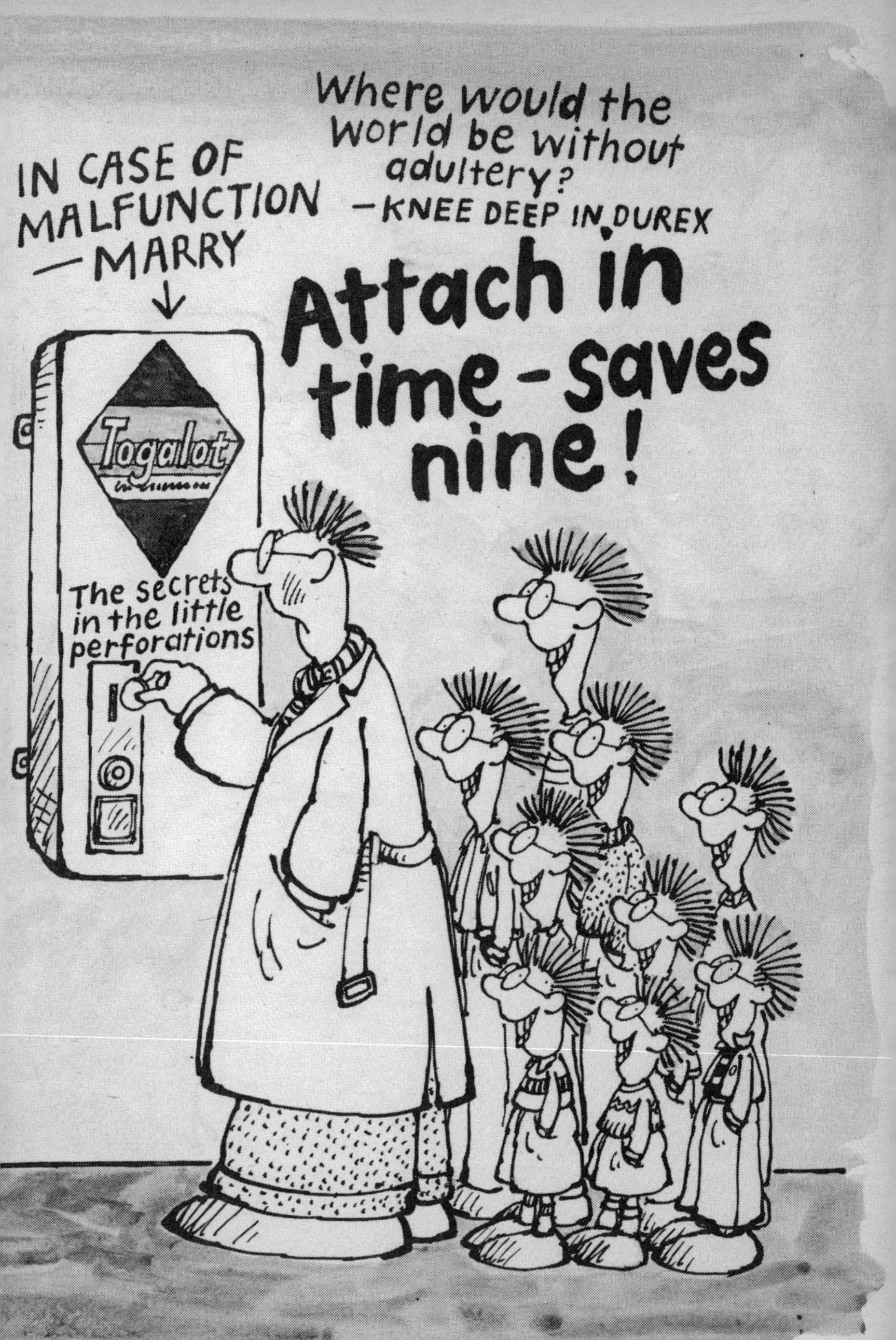

Where would the world be without adultery?
— KNEE DEEP IN DUREX

IN CASE OF MALFUNCTION
— MARRY

Attach in time – saves nine!

Togalot

The secrets in the little perforations

Graffiti's days are numbered – the writing is on the wall!

Make Love – Not War!

REALITY IS A CRUTCH!

Death is hereditary

WHEN IN DOUBT – WORRY

MARRY AND DO BOTH

CHASTE MAKES WASTE

Leda loves swans!

BIGGLES

BE CHAIRY OR YOU'LL FIND YOU'RE SITTING ON A POUFFE

OK sauce rules – HP?

Van Gogh was ear

PRINCESS ANNE FOR MARE

CALL IT INCEST BUT I WANT MY MUMMY!

Destry Rides Again – Why?

DYSLEXIA RULES – KO?

BO PEEP DID IT FOR THE INSURANCE

TRANSVESTITE FOOL – OK.